ROSIE'S SWEAT BOX

ROSIE'S SWEAT BOX

MARKING TIME TILL HOME

David Rozzell

To the crews and families of the World War II heavy-bombing groups of the 8th Air Force.

FOREWORD

Extraordinary—yet typical of the unimaginable modesty and quiet heroism of combat soldiers—is the fact that David Rozzell (himself a combat veteran of the Vietnam War) knew his father, Woodville Grady Rozzell, as a US Air Force pilot during World War II only through photographs and "snippets" related to him through friends and relatives.

Providentially, however, what Grady kept silent about his war experience, he recorded in a diary spanning his very first day in the service in 1943 until he left the combat theater, and eventually departed England for home, in late 1944. The yield of this utterly remarkable diary is *Rosie's Sweat Box*, a candid, expertly documented, brilliantly written, eyewitness account of an Appalachian boy's odyssey through a legendary war from which he emerges, freshly twenty-one years old, a changed and burnished man.

Perhaps, like any memorable war story, *Rosie's Sweat Box* is also a love story, the convergence of Grady and Betty Caroline Thomas, a seventeen-year-old young woman who had traveled from her home in LaFayette, Georgia, to Chattanooga, where Grady was then living with his family, to attend business school. Fittingly, they met in church, in 1942, and in the summer of 1943, they were engaged, the wedding initially postponed until after Grady returned from war. Across the United States—across the world—similarly harrowing, heroic, and understated stories were hatching. Likewise, Grady's narrative is similarly understated, though no less harrowing and heroic.

The diary begins the day Grady leaves home and picks up at his first destination: the Air Force Classification Center in Nashville, Tennessee. This inaugural entry is mostly a list of the mundane, endless, and often-boring protocol of being processed into the United States Military. The reader, however, is instantly immersed in Grady's characteristic fortitude and sense of humor: "Tomorrow has promise . . . I'm slated for KP starting at 5:30 a.m." We learn he exchanged letters with Betty, attended chapel—his faith would sustain him throughout his service— and that he experienced the first tinges of homesickness.

From Nashville, he headed for Maxwell Field in Montgomery, Alabama, and basic training. Grady gives a daily account of his incessant regimen, a nonstop litany of enlightening and dull, thoroughly exhausting, but absolutely necessary routine: physical and intellectual examinations; time on the firing range; PT; the boyish chatter of his comrades about women, food, and back home. Looming over all of this seeming innocence is an unthinkable inevitability: a raging war and certain death for a number of them. The ever-present thread that informs Grady's diary, from the first page to last, are his thoughts of and love for Betty.

Grady's charming, compelling voice, his sense of humor, drive this narrative. The matter-of-fact candor, the understatement, and clear-eyed patriotic idealism that underscores Grady's reflections is rather astonishing. He is passionate to serve his country in the direst way in a deadly war. When we first encounter him, he is a nineteen-year-old boy, still over six months shy of his twentieth birthday.

What's more, this diary is a chapter and verse primer on flight training during World War II, an absolutely indispensable record, replete with a date-and-time line, of archival and historic significance of what it was really like. We learn of Grady's misgivings and exhilaration as he endures hundreds of hours of grueling, intricate, and dangerous training; the entirely new world unfolding around him; his first landing; first solo flight; his unabashed love of flying; his joy at receiving letters from Betty and his mother; and the humble musings of a kid away from home for the first time: "I've just come back from church."

We are with Grady when he proclaims: "HAPPY BIRTHDAY,

ROSEY. You're twenty years old now, boy. Old age has just about got you." Just a bit over a month later, he declares: "I am now a second lieutenant in the Army Air Force. Graduating from twin-engine advanced school at Moody Field, Valdosta, Georgia, October 1, 1943." By the time he notches his first anniversary in the army, he had spent 350 hours in flight training. His yearning for home and Betty is palpable.

Despite plans to wait until after the war to marry, Grady was convinced that he and Betty should marry before he left the states for Europe, and she consented. Betty was still too young to negotiate the necessary paperwork for marriage, so her father had to sign off. She traveled by coach, with two friends, from LaFayette to Tampa, Florida, and on February 23, 1944, she and Grady were married at noon in the chapel at Drew Field Air Force Base.

Their wartime romance and subsequent marriage, with the backdrop of a world in deadly peril, embodies that cinematic sweep often portrayed in those often-sentimentalized vintage '40s war films where couples—by today's standards still kids (Grady was twenty and Betty seventeen)—had just a moment to pass a farewell kiss on the tarmac after their wedding before the man is swept off to combat. In truth, they actually had two months together before Grady's departure. Their maturity, their optimism, and ironclad resolve against all that faced them and the world are astonishing—not to mention the heartache of what would be a long separation.

By early May, Grady was stationed at Deenethorpe AAF Station in Northamptonshire. He announced on the thirtieth of that month, in his characteristic understated aplomb, his first mission: "Well, it looks as though this is it! We're assembled here at the plane, all set to start engines for our first combat mission." After this, the tone and tenor of Grady's diary entries would change appreciably.

His fifth mission was June 6, 1944—D-Day. "I've just returned from a raid to Caen, France. We flew right over the top of the invasion . . . Those boys need all the help we can possibly muster out for them. I'm ready to fly until I drop. Any altitude or any time . . . There's going to be many a good man killed today. Blessing on them."

Noting the mission on the following day, June 7, Grady notes, with decided regret, even helplessness: "There's going to be hundreds of innocent civilians meet their destiny, but this is war I suspect."

Indeed, the more Grady flies, the cost of war, and the notion of mortality, become manifest in his diary. While he continues to relate the day-to-day, like his fellow soldiers having too much to drink, he also becomes understandably preoccupied with the precarity and unpredictability that he's snared in—by then he's seen death and destruction up close—and confides, at one point: "I feel all out of place tonight. I'm lonely, sad, and blue."

After a mission to Bordeaux, France, on June 19, 1944, he prefaces his entry with, "Brother, I'll live a long time before I forget this day." He then goes on to choreograph a particularly terrifying set of circumstances that would repeat itself all too often: ". . . flak slapping the ship like hail against a tin roof . . .

"A piece of flack burst the side window and shattered the side of the left nose gun. Another piece came right down by my head . . . A piece of flak hit Burnett's gun and tore the side off it . . . We had a hole through #1 gas tank . . . I went to see Capt. Hardesty, flight surgeon, tonight. He gave me some sleeping pills for the boys when we need them. We're nervous and scared."

He flies an unbelievable fifteen missions in a span of twenty-four days, and it clearly begins to take its toll: "Won't this ever end?" he laments. "I'm just about done for." For protection, he flies with a "little testament or the little colorful ball that Betty gave [him]."

Providentially, he's granted leave to London and attends a church service at Westminster Abbey, "a quaint and ancient place" where "[e]verything had a death-like appearance." He avails himself of communion while there, and mentions how strong the wine was.

As the frequency of his missions mount—in "Rosie's Sweat Box," as he takes to calling his plane—Grady recounts habitual death-defying experiences with almost numb detachment: engines shot up and literally going out; wings porous from flak. In one instance, his cockpit shatters, and there's a "gaping hole" in the fuselage. There's one near-miss of his body after another. He watches his friends and their planes blasted to bits in midair about him—notably Grady's classmate, and "close buddy," Robert Sproul. Grady admits, "I'm really getting old with these missions. They're flying me too often. This flying and flak are getting me down. I've had enough of this crap. I'm ready for some rest. I want to get my missions in, but I want to be able to walk after I finish." He follows up with, "I hope I can forget this stuff. I'll never be able to though. A fellow will never forget those planes spinning and burning . . . I'm really sweating out the last few missions. I've never been so worried in my life. I can see the end so clearly now. I mean, we're sweating . . . I'm glad we just have two more missions to go."

On Wednesday, August 9, Grady flew and safely completed his thirty-third and final mission. Contrary to the elation he thought he'd experience, he has "a feeling of uneasiness" and is unable to relax. He can't fathom that he'll no longer have to "sweat out flak and fighters, fight a big box of an airplane to keep in formation for nine or ten hours." As he says, "I don't like to sit back and watch the other fellows go out, but I've seen enough"—once again his modesty and gift for understatement at play, but also his fatigue and remorse. In a mere two months and nine days, he had, unimaginably, flown thirty-three missions.

Back in England, preparing to return home, he observes that his fellow soldiers "don't look as young and fresh as the boys we came over with." Then he runs into a classmate of his from Hendricks who informs him that the entirety of his friends from Hendricks had been killed or shot down. He observes, "I suspect this is all the price of war. Very expensive though." Then, a few sentences later, he quips wryly, "...in four days I will have reached the ripe old age of twenty-one. Yes, sir, I'm just about to grow up. Just right for the draft." Only twenty-one, forever changed by what he had seen and endured, he had been to hell and back again and again.

Woodville Grady Rozzell returned home to the Chattanooga area and rather seamlessly picked up his former life and quietly, though memorably, distinguished himself as a devoted husband, father, citizen, and churchman—in fact, a Renaissance man, seemingly gifted in everything, including carpentry, animal husbandry, and athletics. He also completed, through evening classes at the University of Chattanooga, a degree in mechanical engineering and maintained his patriotic fervor by flying for the Tennessee National Guard.

By all accounts, however, he remained relatively silent about his intrepid service as a pilot during World War II. Thank goodness, however, that what he could perhaps not bear to share in conversation, he committed to paper. His diary is an invaluable and intimate document that bears witness in eloquent, often poetic, always candid, and clear-eyed prose to what it was like to defy death daily, in face of overwhelming odds, in midair, thousands and thousands of meters from the earth, for selfless love of country. What a glorious man. What a glorious life.

—Joseph Bathanti
North Carolina Poet Laureate (2012–2014)

INTRODUCTION

I am among all people most blessed in many ways. The biggest blessing was to have had Woodville Grady Rozzell as a father. We shared a neighborhood and life events as long as we both lived. The one event we both knew much too well was war and combat far from home. That is the one experience we never spoke of.

I knew that Grady, my father, had been a pilot and a member of the US Air Force in the big war from the photos I saw around the house, and because he still flew planes for the Tennessee National Guard until I was out of high school. What I learned of his experience I picked up from relatives and friends who had gotten snippets from him. The bulk of the information I have of Grady's war experience comes from his diary to which he religiously confided. He started the daily recordings of his thoughts, fears, and events both routine and extraordinary beginning February 4, 1943—his first day in the military—and continued to contribute daily until he left England and combat.

In 2005, Mike Baldwin, a neighborhood friend, convinced Grady to sit and read from the diary while he videoed him. The filming was an attempt to have Grady add commentary to the diary as he read it. The video disks have been an aid and comfort.

Time and experience can change what a person judges to be fact. People rarely know exactly why events go as they do. Huge in his life were circumstances over which Grady had absolutely no control. He was born August 26, 1923, in the coal mining town of Doyle, Tennessee. Doyle is in White County where David Lansdon Rozzell, Grady's paternal granddad, came in 1873. David Lansdon, his sons, and grandsons worked in the coal mines there until the early 1920s. Because of an economic downturn, most of the mine workers had to relocate to find work. Grady's dad, Frank, his granddad, Edwin, their extended family, and close friends moved to Chattanooga, to where there was a need for carpenter and construction workers. That was how Grady became a resident of the East Lake Community of Chattanooga, Tennessee, before his second birthday.

Grady's mother, Louisa, was a Savage. The Savage family moved to White County in 1803 from Martin County, North Carolina. There remains a strong Savage presence in the White County area. The residents of White County were primarily engaged in agriculture or building trade. The Savage family were farmers but would turn their hand to carpentry when it was available. The few who sought work in Chattanooga with the Rozzell clan maintained a White County residence and loyalty.

Grady lived in the East Lake Community of Chattanooga from his first year until he left to join the war effort. Most of his activities outside the home were centered around the church and specifically the East Lake Church of the Nazarene at 4009 Twelfth Avenue. Grady's parents and grandmother, Willie Elkins Rozzell, were charter members of the church. Grady and his parents lived next door at 4011 Twelfth Avenue.

Grady excelled in athletics. His youth baseball teams were always among the best in the Chattanooga area. In 1936 his team, the Midgets team, won the city tournament. Grady played first base in the final game. He batted four times, had two hits and scored two runs, and was given credit for ten putouts. At Central High, he lettered in track and was city champion in the pole vault. He suffered lifelong knee pains for his efforts. He was jumping ten feet with a bamboo pole and landing in a ground-level pit of sawdust.

He was a member of the high school ROTC. His only real comment to me concerning his ROTC experience was that he liked being a member because he was issued a uniform and, in his words, "got to wear new pants to school." The experience did help when he entered the US Army Cadet program. His accomplishment bio next to his senior picture in the 1941 *CHAMPION*, the school's annual, listed, "entered from East Lake Junior High, 1938," "Bible club." He did have the certificate from the Central High School Athletic Association, which awarded Grady Rozzell the block C letter in track for the season of 1941.

I asked him once why he did not play baseball at Central. He said it was just too hard to get from East Lake to downtown for all the practices. In school, he did excel in all things involving mathematics and the woodworking shop, where he made a couple of library tables still in use by the family.

Grady graduated from Chattanooga Central High School in the class of 1941. The US had not declared war but few doubted that it would happen soon. Grady had decided to attend the University of Chattanooga and study engineering. To earn enough money to cover tuition, Grady worked the summer and early fall with his father and family as a carpenter. Always on his mind was the war and what would be his part in the effort. Of course, later that year, the Japanese attacked Pearl Harbor, war was declared immediately, and the army had an all-consuming need for young men. He told me once, "By the middle of 1942, four men from my graduating class, which numbered one hundred forty-four, had lost their lives in the war effort."

On September 16 of 1940, the country had initiated the first draft of civilians in the US Army in preparation for the coming war. The age limits for registration were twenty-one to thirty-six. This law did not immediately affect Grady. His mother would never have allowed his father to sign the paper necessary for Grady to join if he had been so inclined. He made plans to join the service in a field of his own choice.

Grady had been to the local airport a few times and had a desire to learn to fly. He discovered he could join the Army Reserves and be in line to fill the next available position for flight training. On July 7 of 1942, he enlisted in the Reserves with a promise that he would be taken into the Corps of Cadets (AAFCC) in early 1943 and, if he qualified, become a pilot in the Army Air Corp. He continued his work with his dad and took other jobs, the best of which was a part-time position with the US Post Office, continued his studies at UT Chattanooga, and waited.

MY HERO

by Andrew Tyson
October 4, 2001

My hero is my mom's father, my grandpa. He is my hero
because he saved America. He flew a B-17 Flying Fortress in
World War II. A B-17 is a plane that has four engines
with propellers and can drop bombs. He was a pilot.
My grandpa's name is Grady Rozzell and his plane was named
Rosie's Sweat Box. My grandpa flew thirty-five missions over
Germany and France. I like to look at all of his medals
and pictures of his plane and sometimes he tells me about
the war. He is still alive today and I am proud of him.
I love him.

BETTY

Betty Caroline Thomas
at seventeen years old

One common thread to the story of a young man and a war effort is the attachment to a girl. Grady's story was no exception. His lady was the lovely Betty Caroline Thomas of LaFayette, Georgia. Betty had come to Chattanooga to attend business school.

Betty graduated from LaFayette High School in the spring of

1940. She went immediately to work at The Big Friendly department store in Trion, Georgia. Trion was a cotton mill town. The town had a small hospital, a train station, river, the Riegel Cotton Mill, which produced mostly denim cloth, and a glove factory.

The Big Friendly was the company store, and kind of like the mall we have today. It had a drug store, groceries, general clothing, hardware, shoe department, and food market downstairs. The second floor had offices, ladies ready-to-wear, a ten-cent department, furniture, caskets, buttons, thread, and other sewing supplies.

After high school, Betty worked there in the ladies ready-to-wear department six days a week, seven a.m. to seven p.m. She was paid $14 a week for her efforts.

Sometime in the late summer of 1941, Betty, her mother, and her dad took a coach to downtown Chattanooga for an interview with the president of Edmonson Business School. The school was located on the second floor of a building on Market Street, close to the Miller Brothers Department store. The Edmonson Business School tuition was $100 for a year's schooling in typing, shorthand spelling, and bookkeeping. There was an additional year of classes offered in advanced subjects which included all the big machines used in banks and major schools. Betty did not go that far.

The school year Betty was to attend started on the first of January, '42. The Pearl Harbor attack of December 7 of 1941 changed many things but not her determination to attend business school. Several of Betty's friends and Thomas's cousins were drafted or enlisted immediately. Her best friend was killed later in the battle of Iwo Jima.

Betty had an aunt Flora who was living in Chattanooga. Flora had moved to Chattanooga from Rome, Georgia, in the early 1930s to find work. In 1940, she moved back to Rome. Flora's mother, Mrs. Davis, continued to live on Dodds Avenue in the East Lake section of Chattanooga to care for a cousin, her granddaughter, and Flora's daughter, Dorothy, who wanted to stay in Chattanooga and finish school. Betty knew Dorothy well. After a short discussion, Betty was asked to take a room with Mrs. Davis and Cousin Dorothy so she could attend Edmonson Business School. Aunt Flora had a car and drove Betty to Chattanooga when she moved.

Betty arrived in East Lake on a Sunday morning. Cousin Dorothy attended a church a block or so away from her home and Betty attended Sunday night service with Dorothy that first night. It was the same church Grady attended. Betty sat across the aisle from him but did not remember seeing him. As she knew "what was important," Betty did remember what she was wearing. Her description was, "The dress was a Doris Dodson designer dress, mint green crepe, the shade that made my eyes look so green. I paid five dollars for the dress and I was making fourteen dollars a week. The dress was straight and it fell just below my knees. The bodice had covered buttons almost to the waist and two pockets that had dogwood appliques. I had on low heel shoes, one and one-half inches bone-color Connie Shoes, was carrying a tan clutch that was about six inches by ten inches, and a tan, crocheted, close-fitting beret with three small 'pompom' balls on top." She admitted further that she didn't know how she had met him "but he did follow us home."

Betty was to see more of Grady that night. She said, "I remember later being on the front porch with Dorothy and he came flying down Twelfth Avenue in his car, whipped around the corner onto Dodds Avenue, waving and blowing his horn."

While explaining their early relationship, she said, "Grady invited me to Kay's Ice Cream Parlor for a fudge Sunday and he walked me home from church several times. He gave me the first kiss one night after walking me home from church."

Betty lived only a month with Cousin Dorothy on Dodds Avenue. Her aunt Flora found a house near her home in Rome, Georgia, and moved her mother, Mrs. Davis, there.

The president of Edmonson Business School had put her on

the waiting list at the Frances Willard Home for Working Girls and Betty was able to move there. The Willard House was at 615 Lindsey Street, which was only four blocks from her school. As she described, it "was a lovely home. It had a large parlor available to all. There were strict rules about men being out of the house by ten p.m. I had a nice roommate, a telephone in the hall, and a bath at the end of the hall. The rent was $6.75 a week with breakfast and dinner included." Betty kept crackers and peanut butter in her room for lunch.

Betty worked while she was in school. Her first part-time job in Chattanooga was with W. T. Grant, the five-and-ten-cent store. She worked in the fabric department. She had learned to sew at an early age and was an excellent seamstress. Betty had worked in the fabric and ready-to-wear department at The Big Friendly so brought experience. At W. T. Grant, Betty was paid twenty-five cents an hour and worked four hours every afternoon and all day Saturday.

Early in January, Betty was in typing class. The teacher had turned the radio on for the class to hear President Roosevelt speak. After his speech, government draft-board officials were to draw the first draft numbers. They drew the first number and read it. A lady in the class screamed and fainted. Her son was born on the date of that first number. There were a few men taking the classes but she did not remember any of their reactions.

Betty never really talked about the classwork, her performance grade, or her class standing. I am witness to her speed on the typewriter. As with other tasks, she was quick and accurate. I have one certificate dated 26 June of 1942 in which Betty Thomas is awarded the Penmanship Certificate for Proficiency in Business Writing under instructions of R. V. McCoy.

Betty's story continued, "Edmonson School moved, in the spring, up one block to Walnut Street. We were still on the second floor but a block closer to home. I also took a job at Newells Clinic and Hospital. I worked the switchboard at night from six till ten and Saturday from eight a.m. till six p.m. On weekdays at ten p.m., I wired it up to the third floor and the RNs on that floor answered all the calls. After I left on Saturday, the RNs answered until Monday a.m. The payday was better but I don't remember the amount."

Christmas of 1942, Betty went home to Center Post. Betty's father, Carlos Thomas, had given her a dollar to get her mother a Christmas gift. She found a pair of leather gloves she liked and, after adding a little money to his dollar, bought them for her mom. Betty said simply, "She was pleased with them."

Betty said of that Christmas, "Mother cooked a late breakfast of sausage, country ham, eggs, and biscuit that I really enjoyed. My brother Joel, his wife, Amy, and daughter Nancy were there."

The war effort made life difficult. Betty said little of the hardship, only that "we were very aware of the war shortages, gas was rationed, sugar, meat, even two pairs of leather shoes a year were allowed. The army needed the leather for combat boots."

The summer of 1943 was busy and eventful for Betty. She was able to spend time with Grady who was attending classes on the campus of the University of Chattanooga located a few blocks from her rooming house. Grady was not a resident student. There were city transit buses that went to his residence in the east of Chattanooga. Grady worked at the downtown post office when they had part-time needs, so was often near Betty.

Betty visited Grady's parents and went to church with them on a regular basis. It is safe to say that Betty was not Grady's mother's first choice as a wife for her only son. Louisa, Grady's mother, had picked a girl named Ruby to fill that position. By midsummer, the family did accept Betty as their newest member.

Betty was able to visit her mother and father more than I would have thought. The TAG (Tennessee-Alabama-Georgia) Railroad maintained a rail line from Chattanooga to Birmingham since 1911 to supply Alabama with coal and bring steel back to Tennessee. The company ran a small daily passenger service on the track which the local people called the "Scooter." The Scooter did not follow a firm time schedule. The car carried mail, and while there were no designated stops through the countryside of North Georgia, if a resident waited by the track the train would stop and, for a small fee, take them to any destination on the line. Betty's parents lived a little less than a mile from the track and it was an easy walk to the house.

Betty took Grady to meet her parents for the first time on the Scooter. Grady and Carlos shared an interest in baseball and horses so there was an instant bond there. Mrs. Thomas—I don't remember him ever calling her anything else—was happy to have her daughter happy. As an extended family, we all called her Granny Tom. I asked her once what Carlos had called her and she told me simply, "Oh, he always called me 'Honey.'"

Sometime midsummer, Frank, Louisa, and Nancy Rozzell drove Betty and Grady to Center Post to meet the Thomas family. As far as I know, the meeting went well.

In November of 1942, the draft laws were changed. The new law required all men between the age of eighteen and thirty-seven to register. This brought additional concerns because the change meant that Betty's brother Joel Clayton Thomas would likely be drafted and taken into the war. Joel was taken on July 11, 1943, just five days after Grady enlisted into the Reserves.

Betty Returns
Home to Wait

When actual plans and firm dates were established for Grady to train and then likely participate in the war, Betty prepared for the future. She states plainly that Grady had "chased her since they first met and that she finally said yes." The actual date when she said yes was, even in her words, vague. "Somewhere during the summer ('43) we became engaged, it was hot weather and we were sitting on the glider at 4011 Twelfth Avenue when he asked (again). I finally said yes, not really sure even then." There was not a date set and it was assumed the wedding would not take place until after Grady's war involvement issue was resolved.

Betty decided to return to LaFayette and be with her mother and dad to endure the separation wars presented all couples. She told Edmonson Business School, Newell Clinic, and the Willard House her plans. She then went with her future mother-in-law and sister-in-law to put Grady on the train to cadet school on February 4. Betty then packed her clothes, walked to the bus station, where she caught the afternoon bus to LaFayette. With the help of a friendly neighbor, she was home by dinner.

Betty "had friends in LaFayette who were working to get me a job with the Welfare Department. The job was to be available February first. I did get the job and they gave me an extra week to see Grady off to training and get moved back home. It was a very sad time that we have never forgotten. We always plan something special on that date."

Betty started work "the next morning" in the Welfare Department of Walker County, which was housed in LaFayette. She had a neighbor named Gertrude Thurman who worked at the bank in LaFayette. Gertrude offered her a ride to work. Her best friend Violet worked across the hall in the courthouse. The job "amounted to typing reports that one or the other of the social workers brought to me in script."

We don't know why Grady felt the need to keep a detailed account of his military experience. He did not keep any records of his work, church, or family experience after the war was over. We are fortunate to have the record of his encounters, adventures, and escapades, which start here.

This car was a 1934 black convertible. Grady paid sixty-five dollars for it. Gas cost twenty-five cents a gallon in Chattanooga in 1942, and he confessed that he would never drive it faster than forty-five miles per hour because he was saving his tires, which were rationed at the time.

Diary Begins

February 4, 1943, 7:30 a.m.:

One hour ago, I left my home in Chattanooga, Tennessee. I am now aboard the train going to Nashville, Tennessee, to be classified for training in the US Army Air Corps. I was accompanied to the train by my young sister, Peggy, my pastor Rev. M. L. Garrett, and my girlfriend, Betty Thomas of LaFayette, Georgia.

Outside, the dawn is breaking, the dull gray of which coincides with my gloomy feelings.

12:20 p.m.: Arrived at Nashville. Now to get out to the Air Force Classification Center.

8:40 p.m.: Well, I'm at camp now. We arrived by army truck from Nashville. What a ride! I dread going to bed tonight. I didn't bring bed clothes. I can imagine how those wool blankets will feel on bare limbs. I'd certainly like to see some people I know tonight but "I'm in the army now."

Thus I say finis to my first day in the service.

February 5, 11:00 a.m.:

This morning is slowly dragging by. Inactive except for the occasional detail task. I found a friend, "Leggit" from Mississippi.

I like to have froze last night. The boys from Florida are lambasting this dear state.

8:00 p.m.: I've just returned from the showers. Everyone is talking;

the boys in the adjacent cot are playing cards. Nothing happened today except fingerprinting. Tomorrow has promise though. I'm slated for KP starting at 5:30 a.m.

February 6, 9:00 p.m.:

Tonight I'm a veteran KP. Yes, sir! I've done everything from mopping to dishing out chow.

I got processed this evening. Expecting to get uniform Monday. Got my return address today. Makes me very happy. Now I get letters from Betty and home. Goody!

Sergeant just came through announcing lights out at 10:00 p.m. There's a lot of discussion of women and etc.

February 7, 9:30 a.m.: Sunday morning.

We are all lying around in the barrack. I've just finished reading in the Nashville paper that my school, University of Chattanooga, has been approved for training of aviation cadets. Wouldn't I like to be there.

9:40 p.m.: *I attended chapel tonight at seven o'clock. Had a good service; everyone's in a cheerful mood tonight.*

February 8, 8:20 p.m.:

The boys are discussing the physical examination tonight. We look like soldiers. We were issued uniforms today. We were moved to our permanent barracks today.

Our old southern crew was separated. We got a little bunch of southerners in our end of the building. The boys are very frank in their opinion of the so call "Damn Yankee."

February 9, 8:20 p.m.:

Everything is very quiet tonight. Almost everyone has gone to the show.

I'm very happy tonight. I received two letters, one from home and one from that darling Betty. I love them both.

We had a little foot drill today. I have finished reading the book of Matthew in the Testament Betty gave me. The last verse says, "I am with you always, even unto the end of the world." Amen!

February 10, 9:00 p.m.:

Everything is noisy tonight. It is snowing outside and the Florida boys are really excited.

We were issued our athletic uniforms today. I got to go to the PX tonight. Received a letter from Mother today.

February 11, 9:45 p.m.:

Well, tomorrow is the big day. We start taking our psychological test. I sent my civilian clothes home today. I've tried for the last two hours to call home but no good.

February 13, 9:00 p.m.:

We finished the second day of our test today. Tomorrow, Sunday, we start our physical exams. It has snowed all day.

February 14, 9:40 p.m.:

It's really cold. We nearly froze. Had part of physical examination this morning. NEEDLES! Went to chapel tonight. I have to have a re-check on my X-ray tomorrow. Boy, I hope nothing's wrong.

February 15, 9:00 a.m.:

I have just returned from physical. Everything's okay except my teeth. I've got to have one pulled in the next three days. I think I'll go call Mother. Several have colds.

9:00 p.m.:

The boys are really hilarious tonight. They're having fun out of one of the boys.

Guess I'll go tomorrow and have my tooth pulled.

I wrote Betty a nine-page letter. Called home this morning and talked to Mother.

February 16, 8:00 p.m.:

Well, I'm minus a tooth tonight. Yes, sir, an army dentist got hold of me today. I'm disappointed. I didn't hear from Betty. Mother sent me Betty's picture. Received today.

February 17, 9:15 p.m.:

Well, it warmed up a little today. We went to two lectures today. We've started taking calisthenics. Had the sweetest letter from Betty. She's a darling.

February 18, 9:00 p.m.:

We've been really busy today. I got my first GI haircut this morning.

February 19, 9:00 p.m.:

It's getting tougher and tougher. I love it all. I've got KP Sunday.

Some of the boys are getting classification as navigators. They are disappointed. Had gas drill this p.m.

February 20, 9:00 p.m.:

Oh boy, am I happy. I just finished talking to Betty. Whew, I wish I could see her.

Some more of the boys got classified. Maybe I'll know something tomorrow. I've got KP tomorrow.

February 21, 9:00 p.m.:

Oh, boy! Am I happy. I've been classified as a pilot. I'm so tired from KP I can hardly sit up. I flew the China Clipper today (dish-washing machine).

February 22, 8:00 p.m.:

We got out of quarantine. I took two shots this evening — tetanus and typhoid. Called Mother this evening. She might come to see me Wednesday. Signed payroll tonight.

February 23, 10:00 p.m.:

I've been waiting since seven o'clock on a call from Mother. No good. Nothing new today. Calisthenics and gas mask drill.

February 24, 10:30 p.m.:

The boys are just getting in from Open Post. Some of them are kind of woozy. Mother, Father, Peggy, and Aunt Ruth came up to see me tonight. We drove over into Nashville. Nice to see them. Very, very disappointed that Betty didn't get to come. I love her.

February 25, 5:00 p.m.:

I'm off from guard duty. We go on two and off four. I started at two p.m. We received partial pay this evening. This is all the classified pilots expecting shipment were allowed?

February 26, 9:10 p.m.:

Yippee! We are leaving this place, heading to pre-flight. We're to have baggage packed tomorrow, 7:30 a.m. Didn't write Betty tonight for the first time in three weeks

On March 5, 1943, at 2015 hours, Grady made his first entry into a diary as a pre-flight trainee at Maxwell Field in Montgomery, Alabama. He finished a month of basic military training. Basic training is the military way of teaching men to follow and to work with other men of the military choosing and to do so with vigor and enthusiasm. Attention to detail and hard work are the hallmarks of this training, so Grady did not go into the next part of his training lacking, at least, an idea of what was to be expected of him.

The first entry went like this:

March 5, 20:15:

We're just finished scrubbing our room for Saturday inspection. Hard job. I made two 100s on my first two tests. I got some good nut fudge from Betty. Sweet letters too.

March 6, 21:30:

Pretty good day, typhoid shot 16:30. Ah! We got to eat supper "at ease." Quite a treat. Got back some mail from Betty from Nashville. Tomorrow is Sunday. Wish I was in East Lake.

March 7, 21:00:

Busy day, went to chapel this a.m., to code this p.m. Doubt if I will ever learn the stuff. We have a test again tomorrow.

March 8 21:20:

I've just returned from a code review. We're going to have our first check-in code tomorrow. We're going to school in the evenings this week. Taps!

March 9:

We were busy all day. Not a minute to ourselves. Calisthenics were really tough. Had a card from Levere.

March 10, 21:30:

I'm really tired tonight. I've just returned from the registrar's office. I'm trying to get into an accelerated class. I got time to write Betty and home tonight.

March 11, 21:00:

Whew! I wish Sunday would hurry and get here. I'm a tired duck. Started a new course (Customs and Courtesies); hard day. We changed Mess Halls today. Another three miles to walk.

March 13, 09:30:

Ah! It's raining, no drill. Received my qualifying papers to take the test for the accelerated class. The tests are tomorrow. ALL DAY (Sunday).

March 13, 21:00:

Two more shots this evening—tetanus and typhoid. Got my electric razor this evening. The underclassmen were given a dance tonight. I'm studying for the test.

Sunday, March 14, 17:30:

Whew! The tests are all over. They lasted from 08:00 to 15:00. They *were on communications, ground forces, war publications, math, maps, and charts. We'll know the results tomorrow. Mother called this evening. She is going to fix my Income Tax Return. What a relief! I've got a date Wednesday with the dentist!*

March 15, 21:00:

Whew! I made the accelerated class. I'm moving to new quarters in the morning. We went to the gas chamber this evening. The gas was really bad. Tear gas! We were all crying when we left the place. I got a new gas mask; my other smelled of ammonia.

Accelerated Squadron

March 16, 21:00:

After walking for about an hour, we finally found the place. We're located in nice barracks directly across from the hangars. Kinda seems like the Air Corps. There are six boys in this room. Five from A-10. my new address is AAFPFS (P); Accelerated group. Group 3, Class 43-1, Barracks 621. I just can't get used to being an upperclassman. I'll never forget those harassing days (Underclass March 1–15). And just to think about cutting pre-flight in half is almost too much to believe.

March 17, 21:00:

Oh, boy! Are we in for it. This course is going to be tough. Physics, Naval Forces to get started on. We have a test at the end of every hour. Open Post: Saturday 17:50–Sunday 19:50. What a treat. I hope Mother and Betty can come down. I had two teeth filled this morning. One has to be pulled in the morning. Oh! Went over to see P-38s this p.m.

March 18, 09:00:

I've got my tooth out. Whew! I'm excused from all calls but classes today. It has rained ever since we've moved.

21:00: *I called Mother and told her about the open post. I don't know if her and Betty can come yet. I got out of six-word code.*

March 19, 20:45:

I'm really sleepy tonight. I got a telegram from Mother. She will be here (in Montgomery). She didn't say whether Betty was coming or not. I certainly hope so. I'd really like to see her!

Betty on Visit

"Grady's mother called me at work and asked if I wanted to go with her to see Grady for the weekend. I got permission from everyone, packed a bag, took the bus to Chattanooga, where I met her at the train station. We got to Montgomery and were taken to the visitor center near the base, where we were assigned army cots for the night in an open building pretty much full of mothers and girls like us.

"Grady met us after he went off duty and we spent the night and next day visiting. The visitor center had eating places but we took meals in town, at the cafeteria, and mess hall. I remember the visit as short but very good."

Training Resumed

March 20:

We spent the entire morning learning machine gun, sub-machine, pistol, and rifle. It is really raining and open post tonight. I hope Betty and Mother are waiting on me.

March 21, 22:10: Visited by mother and Betty!

Whatta night, whatta day! I've really enjoyed every moment. It was wonderful to see Betty and Mother. We spent Sat. night and Sunday in Montgomery. It all seems like a grand dream, but I suspect it is true. I love Betty. We're waiting to be interviewed by the lieutenant.

March 22, 20:15:

I'm really tired tonight. My knees are aching. I got out of eight wpm code today. I'm having a little trouble with visual. We finished Naval Forces today. Starting Air Forces tomorrow. I'm still doubting that unforgettable weekend. I can't get it off my mind!

March 23, 20:00:

We went to the low-pressure chamber this morning to simulate twenty-eight thousand feet. Had a cross-country run around the airport.

March 24, 21:00:
We ran the obstacle course, took ten wpm code check, usual hard day.

March 25, 21:00:
We went back to the gas chamber this morning for field identification of gasses. I'm tired tonight. We walked fifty miles today (seems like it). Payday today. I'm out of code. I passed ten wpm check yesterday. This week is passing fast. I went over to A-10 to see the boys tonight. Had the final exam in Physics this evening. I made a 100 percent.

March 26, 21:00:
We went to the firing range this morning. We had preliminary firing with (22) rifle. Had Safe Guarding Military this evening. I think I failed it.

March 27, 14:00:
We've been on the firing range all morning. Using the 45 cal. Colt automatic pistol, 30 cal. Springfield rifle, 30 cal. World War machine gun, and the Thompson submachine gun. Today is the last day of academic work at Maxwell Field. We take final exams in Air Forces and Chemical Warfare this evening. The graduation dance is tonight. We have open post tonight and Sunday. We are moving to Dorr Field, Arcadia, Florida, next Wednesday for Preliminary Flight Training.

March 28, 22:00:
Ah! A very easy day. Went to chapel this morning. Spent most of the evening over on the flying field. Received shipping orders tonight.

March 29, 22:00:
We've had another easy day. Had a formal barracks inspection this

evening by Major Banes. Our shipping date has been canceled. Now we don't know when we will leave. I wrote cards to Leslie Phillips, Frank Cross, Miss Bess Stacey, and Charles Gibson. I wrote a letter to Ralph Brown, Aunt Jessee, Mother, and Betty (of course). The boys are out on open post. We're to have it every night.

March 30, 22:00:

Schedule for the day: "calisthenics and mess." Went to the theater tonight to see a picture about the AVG. We're leaving Friday morning. I called Mother this morning.

March 31, 22:00:

We had calisthenics for the last time this morning. I packed my barracks bags for shipping.

April 1, 21:00: April Fool's Day.

Shipped barracks bags this morning, had a short arm inspection this evening. Leaving in the morning, 09:30.

Dorr Field in
Arcadia Florida
and Actually Flying

April 3, 22:00:

We left Maxwell yesterday at about 14:30. Arrived here at Dorr Field this morning at 07:30. This is really a beautiful place, palm trees, shrubbery, one-story white stucco buildings with four cadets to each room. Four of the boys from my old group are in this room—McElroy, Putnam, Sasser. We were issued our "flying toys" this morning.

Boeing-Stearman Kaydet

April 4, Sunday, 20:00:

Oh, boy! Did we have a wonderful day. I played basketball all morning and went swimming this evening. This Florida sun has nearly blistered me.

April 5, 20:30:

We had introductions today. Received class books, met my instructor this evening. He's a really swell fellow. His name is Wudtke. I'm to start my flight training tomorrow at 11:45.

April 6, 21:00:

AT LAST! I've started flying. I flew thirty-five minutes (11:45) this morning. I'm going to like this fine. It's going to be a lot of hard work though.

April 7, 20:40:

We've had a busy day. We spend the entire morning on the flight line and evening in ground school and calisthenics. My ground school subjects are navigation, meteorology, theory of flight, and engine. I flew forty-five min., total 1:20.

April 8, 21:00:

I got forty-five min. more of flying time. I improved a little on coordination but my taxing is rotten. Had four letters from Betty today. Heard from Frank Cross. Had my first forced landing today. I like flying, total 2:05.

April 9, 21:00:

It's pouring down rain outside. Betty and Mother have my new address. Flew thirty-three min., total 2:38.

April 10, 22:30:

Almost everyone has gone on open post. It's really beautiful outside tonight. I wish I could see Betty. I tried to call home tonight but to no avail. I didn't fly today. Bad weather.

April 11, 21:15, Sunday:

Another day of rest. I went to Arcadia to Trinity Methodist Church, played a little tennis this evening. A very pleasant day.

April 12, 21:00:

Started on landings today. Blood type today. We were put on quarantine. No one seems to know why or how long. Time fifty min., total 4:26.

April 14, 22:00:

I'm disgusted tonight. I really did punk in flying today. Landing again with a high wind. I didn't do a thing right. Had a letter from Bowne today. Time fifty, total 5:16.

April 15, 22:15:

I feel a little better about my flying. It's really chilly tonight. Time 1:05, total 6:21.

April 16, 21:00:

Same usual day. Building up my time to nine hours (minimum to solo). Time 1:08, total 7:29.

April 17, 21:40, Saturday:

Quarantine lifted today. Everyone has gone on open post. These

Saturday nights are the most lonesome night of all. It makes me want to go home so bad, it is almost unbearable. I'm supposed to solo Monday. Time forty-five, total 8:14.

April 18, Sunday:

Another pleasant day of rest. I played tennis with Baynes this morning. Missed the bus to Arcadia and didn't get to go to Sunday School. I'm supposed to solo tomorrow if the weather permits.

April 19, 21:45:

I'm disappointed tonight. I didn't get to solo today. No underclass was allowed to solo. We had a storm last night. It rained 1 $1/2$". Time forty, total 8:45.

I had an exceptional sweet letter from Betty. I wish I could see her.

April 20, 20:50:

I'm disappointed again tonight. I still haven't gotten to solo. I didn't even fly today. Maybe tomorrow will be my day. We've had a test in all our subjects. My ground average for last week is ninety-two.

April 21, 21:00:

I finally got to solo. No thrill though. I was just a little uneasy. The plane seems more complete with Wudtke in the front cockpit. Time thirty, total 9:44.

April 22, 21:00:

I soloed again today. I'm supposed to solo from Dorr Field tomorrow. I wrote Ralph and Leland a letter last night. We received our traveling expenses this evening for the trip from Maxwell. Time twenty-two to thirty, total 10:38.

April 23, 20:30:

    I soloed from Dorr Field this a.m. I can check out a plane tomorrow. Our time starts doubling tomorrow. The upperclass are finishing up their flying. We have two tests tomorrow, engines and meteorology. Time twenty to twenty-five, total 11:20.

April 24, 23:00:

    Saturday night and another open post. I'll never forget the day with its mistakes. The first day I checked out a plane. A living memory of disgust. I cut off the gas and plane quits out in the middle of the field. Did I feel little. Then I take off and fly a whole period without fastening my safety belt. Maybe I'll learn. That is, if I get another chance. Time fifty-five to fifty, total 13:01.

April 25, 20:00: Easter Sunday!

    Not at all like any previous Easter. I went to church in Arcadia this morning and slept most of the evening. I've been working on my notebook for the last three hours. The boys are still on open post.

April 26, 21:00:

    I believed that my flying days were over last Saturday. I feel a little better about it tonight. Lt. Mather came in a few minutes ago and wants me to be flight capt. this week. Time fifty.

April 27, 20:20:

    I feel good tonight. Mr. Wudtke told me I might take the twenty-hour check tomorrow. I hope I can pass it. We are going to fly all day tomorrow. I did my first loop today. It is not as thrilling as it looks. I did my first spin by myself today. It took me a long time to make up my mind to twirl that thing at the ground. I did it though. Time thirty five to forty-five.

April 28, 21:05:
Oh, boy! I passed the twenty-hour check. I still don't know how I did it. I had a change in instructors today. I really liked Mr. Wudtke. My new instructor is Mr. Shaw. We stayed on the line all day today. We went over to the academic area tonight to hear the articles of war. Time 25–153, total 10:04.

April 29, 20:45:
I had my first ride with my new instructor today. I'll never forget those words that pounded in my ears, "Increase, increase, increase, RELAX!" He is really going to put some flying to me until I catch up with the rest of his group. All the boys have gone over to the upperclass farewell dance. We started chandelles* and lazy-eights today. Time 2:05–50, total 21:59.

April 30, 20:50:
Payday today. Two planes crashed this p.m. as they were taking off. They were about twenty feet in the air. No one was seriously hurt. Both planes were torn to a wrecked heap. I flew four periods today. My new instructor is certainly strict. Time 2:26–1:05.

May 1, 20:10:
Another lonely, peaceful Saturday night. I flew five hours, ten minutes today, and am I tired. We had a storm this evening. I had an encouraging letter from Betty. I'll never forget these words: "Grady, darling, if anybody can fly, you can fly." If only I had as much confidence in myself. The underclass arrived this morning, which reminds me that I've been here a month today. How time flies. Time 3:05–2:05, total 30:35.

---

* A chandelle is an aircraft control maneuver in which the pilot executes a 180-degree turn while climbing to a higher altitude.

May 2, 22:30:

I've just come back from church. The boys are all in exploiting their miraculous weekends. I got a little too much sun this evening. That darling, Betty, called me this morning. I talked to her, Mother, and Peggy. It was a pleasant surprise when they aroused me this morning and told me I had a long-distance call.

May 3, 20:30:

Oh, me! Everything went wrong again today. I get worse with every hour I fly. Mr. Willis slipped an engine test on us today. I just know I failed. I'm studying for a navigation test tomorrow. I'm about half-sick from the sun. Half of my time is gone here. I hope. Time 2:05–1:05, total 33:49.

May 4, 21:30:

Another bad morning. Mr. Shaw threatened to bring me back to the field to make me write a one-thousand-word theme, and to break my arm with the stick. We are getting ready for forty-hour check. Time 2:10–1:00.

May 5, 19:45:

Ah! No dual time today. I dragged a wing landing crosswind this morning. I know I get worse every hour. They're having a dance for the upperclass tonight so I'm alone.

May 6, 21:05:

Whee! Yippee! I don't see how I did it but I passed my forty-hour check this morning. I had Mr. Wudtke, my former instructor, for the checker. He showed me snap rolls. We're going on our cross-country flight tomorrow. I had my first period in the Link Trainer [†] this morning. Time 55–1:28.

May 7, 20:15:

We had our first cross-country flight this morning. It took one and a half hours.

We went east to Okeechobee City, south to Palm Lake, and back to Dorr Field. Had a sweet letter from Betty. Time 2:20, total 42:20.

May 8, 21:00:

We started acrobatics today. Slow rolls and snap rolls. I did all right with Mr. Shaw but when I tried them solo, I always ended up in a power dive. Tomorrow is Mother's Day. I just wish I could go home to see mine. Time 1:20–30.

May 9, Sunday, 20:30:

Mother's Day, and me, hundreds of miles away from home. I just hope the rest of the Mother's Days will be different and I can be at home. I've slept most of the day. Went swimming and played a little basketball. I wrote letters to Ralph, Levere, Mother, and to Gladys Gandy.

May 10, 20:05:

We are flying in the evening this week. We didn't get to fly much because of the storm threat. Time 1:20, total 46:20.

[†] The Link Trainer was developed by Ed Link and his company, Link Aviation Devices, Inc., in 1929. The flight simulator was initially produced to provide a safe way to instruct pilots in the performance of instrument flight.

May 11, 21:10:

Got back in the groove today. I flew four periods. Took up the rest of my acrobatics this evening. Half rolls, Immelmans,‡ loops. I still haven't got the knack of flying upside down.

May 12, 20:40:

No flight today. We had high wind and threatening clouds. Received a picture of me taken at Maxwell. I put it in the front of this book.

May 13, 20:45:

It will take a long time to forget this miserable day. I have my first thing to do right in my dual flight this evening. Mr. Shaw made me spend the rest of the evening practicing chandelles, pylon, and lazy eights. Time 2:30–1:00, total 51:25.

May 14, 21:00:

I had another hour of Link today. No dual flight. I stayed out too long on my solo period. Time 1:10.

May 15, 17:00:

I'm getting to go to Sarasota. I had a pretty good day today. Time 2:00–1:10.

---

‡ Immelmans are flight maneuvers in which the plane is flown in the opposite direction at a different altitude. The maneuver was used by fighter pilots in WWI to reposition an attacking plane for another attack approach.

May 16, 22:30:

I've really had a swell weekend. I spent the night at Sarasota Hotel. My roommate was Bek. I spent most of the evening on the beach with a buddy from Athens, Tennessee—Shipley. It was the first time I had seen any saltwater. I don't care much for swimming in it. In fact, I'd rather see the hills of Tennessee than all their white-crested waves, and I ain't kidding!

May 17, 20:20:

I was scheduled for my sixty-hour check today but bad weather set in and I'm still on the fence. I hope I can pass it. I've only eight more hours to finish here. Time thirty to thirty-five.

May 18, 19:30:

Am I happy! Am I surprised! I passed my final flight check. All I've got to do to finish is to fly five more hours and take a few finals. Along with the good news, I got some bad news. I've been assigned to Bainbridge, and if the things are true that I hear about the place, it is horrible.

May 19, 19:35:

Well, if nothing happens, I'll finish flying tomorrow and will I be glad. I'm rather anxious to get to Bainbridge. I had a letter from David Neeley.

May 20, 20:05:

They wouldn't let us finish today. I've finished all but twenty-five minutes though. Time 1:00, Link 1:00.

May 21:

I flew for the last time at Dorr Field today. I got to ride in the front cockpit with the instructor in the rear. They call the last ride a "bitch ride." The student gets to be the instructor. We took a final in engines. I made a ninety-six on it. I wrote Leland§ tonight. He is in New York, New York. We had our first blackout tonight. Time twenty-five, total 60:00.

May 22:

I got a release from the flight line this morning. Had another hour of Link. I've got two more hours to go. Link 1:00.

May 23, Sunday:

Am I tired. I really pulled a foolish trick this evening. Truitt, Veillieux, and I slipped over the fence this evening headed for the alligator hole to see the alligators. From the air, the distance didn't look to be over two or three miles. Well, we found out different. After five hours of walking through palmettos and undergrowth, we finally got back to the field. We were two hours late for supper and we haven't seen the alligators yet, except from the planes.

May 24, 22:30:

We had final exams in navigation and meteorology this morning. My roommates are out on open post tonight. Had a sweet letter from Betty!

---

§ Leland "Dabber" Rozzell was Grady's uncle who joined the war effort September 15, 1942. Dabber was now part of the 3rd US Army and headed for Africa and the combat as part of General George Patton's Army.

May 25, 20:15:

Had two more final exams this morning. Theory and army theory and engines test from Maxwell Field. Checked my flying equipment back in this evening.

May 26, 20:00:

Finished exams this morning with an army test in navigation. My parents are moving to Harriman, Tennessee, today. Now I'm without a home. I wish they hadn't moved. **

_____

** On February 2, 1943, Clinton Laboratories (later to be named Oak Ridge National Laboratories) broke ground on a fifty-nine-thousand-acre tract of land in eastern Tennessee. The project was a top-secret operation which brought three thousand construction workers to the area by the summer of 1943. Grady's dad, Frank Rozzell, took a job with them as supervisor of housing construction for the project, and after a short stay in Harriman, Tennessee, moved onto the base and lived in one of the temporary houses, of which he was supervising the construction.

Grady's father, Frank Rozzell, was a patriot of the top shelf. He was too young to participate in WWI. His father would not sign for him to join as a seventeen-year-old, and now his age disqualified him from service in WWII. He was a member of the Home Guard. We have no official paperwork which detail his service but there is one letter in our possession which does confirm his participation. Captain W. M. Richards of Company I, 6th Regiment of the Tennessee State Guard, which was stationed in Chattanooga, wrote Frank a letter of recommendation dated April 6, 1943, addressed to his counterpart, Captain McGinley, in Clinton, Tennessee. It reads:

"One of my best men, Cpl. Frank Rozzell, is leaving Chattanooga shortly to take a job on your big army construction project. Cpl. Rozzell wants to stay in the Guard and will probably apply for enlistment in your company. He will certainly make you a good and my advice to you is to grab him as soon as you see him.

"We hate to lose Frank, but it will be your gain."

May 27, 21:00:

We had an athletic competition over at Carlstrom Field this evening. I played on the basketball team. Dorr won every event.

May 30 (Sunday), 22:40:

We've spent the last two or three days waiting to be shipped. We were scheduled to leave yesterday at 15:00 but plans were changed and now no one knows when we will leave. Soon I hope.

More Basic
Flight Training at
Bainbridge, Georgia

June 2, 21:00:
We left Arcadia last night at about 6:30, ate breakfast in Jacksonville, Florida, arrived here at BAAB at about 3:30 p.m. They told us we were out of the country club now. My first impression is not so good.

June 3, 21:30:
Overslept and missed reveille this morning. Had orientation lectures this morning and met my instructor, 2nd Lt. E. V. Moore. I like him fine. Had my first flight in the BT-15 this morning. Flies like a box car. Time eight.

Vultee Valiant BT-6

June 4, 21:00:
Started ground school and calisthenics this morning. Radio and communication, navigation. Started stalls and spins. Had a sweet letter from Betty. I'm beginning to like this place. Dear state of Georgia. That's where my sweetheart lives. Time 1:00, total 66:08

June 5, 21:00:
These hard days are killing me. They really throw this stuff at us fast. I'm not getting enough sleep.

June 6, Sunday, 20:30:
Got to sleep a little extra this morning. Flew this evening. Received several letters from Dorr Field today. One from Eloise Rozzell and one from my pastor Rev. M. L. Garrett. Time 1:02.

June 10, 21:20:
Am I happy tonight. I soloed the BT-15 today. I've been doing some rotten flying the last few days that I had given up on ever soloing. I am really surprised that there was nothing to it though. I've been so busy this week that I haven't had time to write in my diary. We are going to ground school at night this week. This is really a hard life.

June 13, Sunday, 20:00:
What a swell day. No flying or school. If I just had a week of Sundays like this to rest, I'd feel a lot better. I'm beginning to like this Vultee Vibrator.†† I think we start shooting stages tomorrow. I hope everything softens up a little. It couldn't get much harder.

---

†† Vultee Vibrator is the name given the Vultee B-13 Valiant training plane.

June 14, 21:00:

We shot our first stage today. Capt. Wilson called my first landing a Kangaroo landing.

June 15, 08:20:

They are celebrating the first anniversary of Bainbridge Field today. We didn't have to fly today; I'm glad too. My knees are still aching from holding the brakes so much yesterday shooting the ninety-degree side approach stage.

June 16, 20:00:

We had a thunderstorm this evening. I just had a period of dual. I went into two accidental spins.

June 17, 20:05:

Shot twenty-degree flap stages this evening. I think I did pretty good. I flew with a new instructor today. Lt. Pashley. I don't know whether he will be my regular instructor.

June 18, 21:00:

Had a sweet letter from Betty today. I did a forced landing that almost pleased my instructor today. Scared me. I'll be glad when Mother and Betty can come.

June 19, 20:00:

The boys have gone on open post tonight. We had a parade and inspection this evening instead of flying. Capt. May came by, stepped on my toe, and then came back by inspecting and gigged me for improperly shined shoes. Betty sent me some good fudge candy. I love her. The boys

*have been amusing themselves by talking to the Waac's as they pass on
their way to mess.*

June 20, Sunday, 09:00:

*This is really a beautiful day down here in Georgia. I wish I was
home though. We had to fly this evening. We've been having a big ar-
gument as to whether to fly half-rolls or loops when he lands on the
ceiling. Personally, I think he loops. Again, I wish I could go home.*

June 22, 20:30:

*I'm really tired tonight. However, I'm not as disgusted as I usually
am. I'm beginning to like flying again. I had almost given up hope of
getting through, but now I have more confidence and interest. I've just
got to make good. I received the bad news of the death of one of my
uncles—Edwin Little Rozzell.*

June 23, 21:00:

*Started flying instruments today. First day under the hood. The
plane doesn't fly like the Link Trainer. I started radio in Link Trainer
today. I think I'm going to like it. I almost had a real forced landing
today. I had left the ground on the takeoff and the engine cut off. It
started up though. It tried to quit two more times while I was climbing
to reenter traffic. I was really glad to get on the ground. I ain't fooling
either.*

June 24, 19:30:

*This has really been a hectic day. I had twenty-hour check with Lt.
Bauer (asst. CO). I couldn't even check the mags to suit them let alone
fly. After getting all frustrated by the check, I had to go shoot a sixty-
degree flap stage for Capt. Wilson at Vada Field. I overshot the field*

twice out of six attempts. We were scheduled for night flight tonight, but it was called off because of bad weather.

June 25, 19:00:
   We are scheduled for night flying tonight. I start at 23:30.

June 26, 07:30:
   Am I sleepy this morning. I didn't get to bed until two o'clock this morning. Night flying wasn't so difficult. I made three landings dual, then three landings solo.

June 27, Sunday, 20:00:
   Ah! For a few more days of rest like this—not a chance though. I went to chapel this morning and slept most of the evening.

June 28, 21:00:
   We're flying double schedule until the underclass gets here. I had an instrument spin today. He turned us over on our back and gave the ship to me. The only way I could tell that I was on my back was the fact that I was out of the seat hanging on the belt.

June 29, 08:00:
   Schedule for today: fly this morning, this afternoon, and tonight. We're flying at Vada field tonight. I have a hard enough time landing there in the daytime.

June 30, 21:00:
   Finished flying this morning at four o'clock. I'm just a little sleepy

tonight. I just have two more nights of night flying. I like night flying but I had rather sleep. Payday tonight. I didn't get to fly today because of the weather.

July 1, 20:00:

Started formation flying today. Planes get a little too close for comfort. Maybe I'll get used to it

July 2, 21:00:

We had the forced landing stage today. We circled the field at twenty thousand feet and at the order of control ship, we would cut the gun and try to land. To my surprise, I hit five out of six of the landings. I landed on the grass instead of the runway when I came back to the main field. The tower caught me. I was awarded three stars and had to wear a sign that said, "Gourdhead Dumstunt." We are going on a cross-country flight to Crestview, Florida. My first cross country was to Albany, Georgia, last Tuesday. I had to fly the entire trip under hood.

July 3, 21:30:

It'll be a long time forgetting this day. Capt. Wilson caught Shipley and me flying formation on the return trip from Crestview. As soon as we landed he sent us back to the barracks under confinement and the threat of a court-martial. Rather a sinking feeling. You betcha. We were called to the chief tactical officer's office this evening and was told our punishment would be confinement until Monday morning reveille. We were also told that the next little thing would mean "outs." One of the boys spun in last night. He died sometime today (Shultz). Tomorrow is the Fourth of July, and me, confined.

July 4, Sunday, 13:00:

A lovely day as seen out our barrack's window. I sure am important *to the AAF. They even send the cadet officer of the Guard around every hour to see that I'm still here. Capt. Wilson is really considerate. He's going to let me out to have a parade and have inspection this evening. The seventeen-year-old boys are visiting here this evening. They are trying to influence them to join the cadets. I hope they don't get the wrong impression.*

July 8, 21:40:

What a mess this week has been. I was greeted with a check ride first thing Monday evening when we reported to the flight line. I went with Capt. Wilson. I was scared stiff. I just knew it would be my last ride. I was so disgusted that I didn't care much. I flew accordingly. He said the ride was unsatisfactory and that he would ride with me again. Lt. Moore was really tough on me today. He said he was disgusted with me getting "caught" flying formation. Tuesday: the next day, after I failed the ride with Capt. Wilson, he took me out and tried to teach me stalls and even made me shoot some landings. He was really hot. I went on a team ride with Selch to Arlington, Tuesday. I was under the hood. We flew last Monday night. Had wing light landings for the first time. They tend to make you run the airplane in the ground, which I did. One of my buddies, Ross, tore up the landing gear on a light generator when he took off. It crumpled when he landed. We had formation landings yesterday. We are flying again tonight. The last night! Mother sent me a little radio last night. It's really a killer. We were supposed to have gone on a cross-country this evening but it was called off because of the weather.

July 9, 20:00:

I had another ride with Capt. Wilson today. This one seemed satisfactory though. I had been up solo just previous to flying with him. I did so many chandelles and lazy eights that the shadow of the plane wore a bare streak on the ground

July 10, 21:00:

No flying today. We had a course in chemical warfare this morning and then had an examination on it. We had the usual Saturday personal inspection but no parade. We had a short talk by Col. Savage at the post theater about taking our dependents to operational training.

July 11, Sunday, 21:30:

We had an assembly to hear the Articles of War this morning. I attended the Post Chapel. We had the cross-country flight scheduled but it was called off again. I acted as an observer for Peper on a team ride to Arlington, Georgia. After we had landed and started taxiing back to the line, I looked back and the ship landing behind me was standing up on its nose and landing gear. I got lost twice today in Link, trying to fly a scissor radio range using the fade-out system.

July 12, 21:00:

We had our second cross-country this morning. It was in a triangular pattern. BAAF to Empress, Georgia, to Norman Park, Georgia. Back to BAAF. Lt. Bauer made me get out and see if I had brought in any pine tops when I landed. I was a barracks orderly today. I received my first gig this morning for being late for flight-line formation. Our flight for to stand retreat tonight. A P-38 cracked up today. Landing gear wouldn't let down. We went to ground school tonight but they called it off.

July 13, 21:00:

We were stationed at Vada Field today to shoot hurdles. I didn't get to shoot mine. I went up for a dual instrument ride the first period. I rode in a truck back to the field. I really enjoyed the ride. Such a change. I think trucks are dangerous. Passed my code check in ground school tonight. Santela, Richer, and I went to bowl some but the alleys were filled.

July 14, 20:00:

We went to post-theater this morning to hear crew members of B-26 just back from combat. It was very interesting. They put on an exhibition with two B-26s down on the flight line. I don't like the things at all. I flew solo formation this morning.

July 15, 21:15:

We went on our last cross-country today. BAAF-McRea-Butlrt-BAAF. It took three and a half hours. I was really tired when I got back. I had an interview with Lt. Frauenberger yesterday. It was to determine my rating toward being a flight officer or 2nd Lt. I'll probably be a flight officer, if I'm lucky. Had letter from Eloise Rozzell today.

July 16, 20:00:

We are finishing up with flying. There's a lot of diversified time flying of the end. Today I had a period of dual instrument, a team ride under the hood with Scofield to Blakely, Georgia, and one solo period of acrobatics. I'll be glad when we finish. I'd like to start off with a clean sheet. I've just got to do better in advanced than I've done here at basic. I really got started off on the wrong foot here. I think maybe I'll get through though. I'm beginning to like this plane. I'll be glad to get to advanced and start flying twin-engine jobs.

July 17:

We were stationed at Vada Field again today. I got to shoot hurdles in the first stage. Believe it or not, I made the third-highest score in our flight. Capt. Wilson said, "Nice stage, Rozzell, you are really dropping them in there." I didn't know what to say. It certainly made me feel good, though, to do something right for a change. I had my acrobatic dual ride. We just got two dual rides in acrobatics. Lt. Moore really put me in a sweet sleep today when he pulled out of a split "S." I had *formation landings and takeoffs with Lt. Carr. I rode back to the field in the truck again.*

July 18, Sunday, 21:30:

I've enjoyed this day. I went to chapel this morning. I went off the post on open post for the first time since I've been here. Truthfully, I don't believe I've missed much. I went to town with Saatela. We visited the USO, bowled a couple games, looked the town over, and came back to post. I've been assigned to twin-engine school. We are supposed to leave BAAF July 30 for Moody Field, Valdosta, Georgia, which is located about fifty miles east of here. There have been some heated arguments between the twin- and single-engine boys. They call us taxi drivers for bombardiers. We have a lot of fun ribbing each other. I can hardly wait until next weekend. Betty and Mother are supposed to come. I hope nothing happens to hinder them.

July 19, 21:00:

I took my last instrument ride this morning. I've just got an instrument check now. I can almost see the end of basic now. We were scheduled for our night cross-country but, due to weather, it was called off. We had to go down to the flight line and get a lecture anyway.

July 20, 17:00:

Whatta day. I rode under the hood for two straight hours then rode as an observer the next hour. My buddy was Shipley, the boy I was caught flying formation with. I had a solo period of acrobatics too. We're flying tonight.

July 21, 20:00:

I finally got to go on my cross-country last night. It was called off temporarily because of the weather. I left at 00:30. It took two and a half hours to make the flight. We went to Dothan, Alabama, to Troy, Alabama, to Marianna, Florida, then back to Bainbridge, Georgia. I made a perfect landing back at the home field. My first good landing at night. I was awakened this morning to go to the flight line for my in- strument check and last hour of acrobatics. It was so late when I got there that I only flew the period of acrobatics. Lt. Bauer said he would call me tomorrow morning and give me my check. Everyone else has finished but me. C flight won first place in the field day. I was on the scrub team for hurdles but didn't get to fly. I was really scared once last night when I ran into a cloud. The red passing light made a solid red wall. I just knew my day had arrived, but I'm still here.

July 22, 21:00:

Whee! I've finished flying at basic. I'm so happy I don't know what to do. Lt. Bauer gave me my instrument check this morning. I'd never even thought about finishing here with the start I made, but everything has turned out okay. C flight had a picnic over at the officers' athletic field this evening. We had a fairly nice time. I said farewell to Lt. Moore this evening. I received a letter from Rev. M. L. Garrett.

July 23, 08:30:

I'm in a pickle of a shape this morning. Our whole barracks slept through reveille and breakfast this morning. Mother and Betty are com- ing tomorrow too. So if something don't turn up, Rosey will be walking tours with them in town. Now, ain't that awful? We're going to ground school double schedule today (meteorology).

July 30, 06:30:

What a wonderful time I had this weekend. Mother and Betty came Saturday and stayed until Tuesday night. I've been floating around in the air ever since they left. This week had certainly passed fast. I wrote Dabber a letter last night. He is over in Sicily. I wish I was over there to help him. At last, we are leaving this place. I've got all my bags packed and ready to be carried down to HQ. I never dreamed of getting through here, but when I look back it really hasn't been so tough. Now Rosey, if you can only make advanced. Luck to you, old boy. Something tells me I'm going to need it. Valdosta here we come.

ADVANCED TWIN-ENGINE FLIGHT TRAINING, VALDOSTA, GEORGIA

July 30, 21:30:

We arrived here about 16:00 this afternoon via GI trucks. What a ride. I believe I'm going to like it here swell. They seem to have a little organization and know what's going on. They said they had the best and most food here. It can stand a large improvement over BAAF.

We must take a physical examination before we start flying. I hope I'm in tip-top condition. The quarters are a large improvement over BAAF's one-story barracks. These are double-deckers and divided into rooms with three cadets to a room. My roommates are Saatela and Ross. I spent most of the evening trying to get my belongings straightened out. Everything's in a mess. We had strawberry malt for beverage at supper tonight. This couldn't be the army.

Once again I'm in the bewildered state of starting off at a new station. It's really a peculiar feeling. One of anxiety mixed with the dread of something new. I've learned in these almost six months of army life not to dread, but wait patiently. I believe I spent two-thirds of the first three months waiting in line. However, I've never had more confidence in myself than I have now. I'm actually eager to start flying. I suspect my enthusiasm will wear out and change to confusion in a couple of days or so when I start in a ship with two engines. It's almost unbelievable that I am at my last station before graduation.

Anyway, I'm frazzling glad of it and I'm really going to do my best. Here. Ah! That's the spirit, Grady.

July 31, 20:40:

Uh! I don't know if I'm going to like this place or not. They certainly started this day off wrong. The first place they sent us was to the dental clinic. I've four teeth to be filled. They issued our flying suit and sunglasses this evening. The suit is nifty compared to the GI coveralls we've been wearing. I've laid around most of the day. We have our sixty-four (physical examination) tomorrow afternoon.

August 1, 20:00:

What a day. It took most of my afternoon to take the physical. Luckily I passed everything okay. I'm all set to start flying now. Tomorrow may be the day. I don't know why, but I'm eager to get started.

August 2, 21:15:

My, my, what long days they have here. I just finished supper a few minutes ago. I met my instructor this morning, Lt. DeLaney. He seems to be a swell fellow! We didn't get to fly today, just got acquainted and gave us a lot of procedures to learn. We have enough stuff to learn tonight. I believe it will take me a month to learn it. We had ground school all evening. It all seems to be instruments mixed with a little navigation. We were introduced to the new Renshaw method of aircraft recognition. It's all right. I have a dental appointment tomorrow.

August 3, 21:30:

I've just returned from the dentist. He almost killed me. Filled seven teeth in just a few minutes. Oh, boy, did I have a darling letter from

Betty. She's the sweetest girl in the world and I know. If any doubts it, they can ask me, and how. I didn't get to fly today, however, I had some Link.

August 4, 21:15:

Well, I've had my first ride in the AT-10. Frankly, I'm disappointed. I've lost all my eagerness in one flight. It's more difficult to taxi than it is to fly. There's just about two hundred too many things to remember for me to fly that thing. I think I can learn in about two months though—I guess, I hope. I went over to look at the officers' uniforms tonight. I have an appointment with the tailor to get measured next Tuesday night. The name of my plane today was "Miss Peggy," my little sister's name.

Beech AT-10 Wichita

August 5, 21:00:

We started takeoffs and landings today. I took off like a drunk man. No, I think a drunk man could have held the ship straighter. It certainly takes a long time to go around the traffic pattern. I can readily see where my next many hours will be spent. That is, if I last long enough to shoot landings. You have to fly this plane. Most of the boys are sick of their choice of advanced schools. We had functional swimming for calisthenics today.

August 6, 21:40:

We were stationed at Bemiss today. I didn't get to fly though. I had to ride over and back in the truck. We had a cross-country run and the obstacle course in calisthenics. They had the best obstacle course of any I've seen. Maybe I should say the worst. I've been here a week today. I hope the days start passing faster. I never get to bed before ten o'clock. Most of the boys are over at the cadet dance. They have a dance every Friday.

We had a code check this afternoon. I didn't get the characters out of the entire check. We're using the Renshaw System of Aircraft Recognition. I missed two ships out of twenty on the first test. I'll never make that good again though, One one-hundredths of a second isn't so much time to identify a plane.

August 7, 20:00:

Woe is me. Will I ever learn how to land this plane? I'd better get learning and learning fast. After we had worked for about two hours this afternoon, getting everything ready for inspection, they announced that the inspection had been called off and that we could leave for open post until tomorrow night. Talk about a bunch of happy boys.

Needless to say, I'm about the only one left here. I'm going to get some muchneeded sleep. Ah!

August 8, 22:15:

What a day. Quiet, peaceful. I've certainly rested this weekend. I went to chapel services this morning. Listened to the radio and read magazines most of the afternoon. I hate for this day to end. I wrote M. L. Garrett, my pastor. I sent a letter to Piper Corporation too. I hope I *have some response from them. I wrote Betty a five-page letter tonight, the longest letter I've written in months. I love that sweet girl.*

August 9, 21:25:

Believe it or not, I'm going to get checked out in the AT-10 tomorrow. We were stationed at Valdosta Municipal Airport today. We twisted a wheel in the asphalt strip when we started to turn around with the brake on one wheel. With the help of about a dozen cadets, we finally got out. The runway was really soft.

I shudder when I think of the little incident that happened today. Lt. Delaney was giving me single-engine landings today. On one of the landings, he cut back the mixture control instead of the throttle. I went on and landed but when I tried to give the gun to clear the runway the left engine didn't rev up. I had made a strictly one-engine landing. It's a good thing I didn't bounce and have to ease it down with one engine. The dead engine was a surprise to both of us. But I'll bet it'll never happen like that again. No, I'm looking as to which little handle is pulled back, believe you me.

August 10, 22:00:

I did it today. Yes, sir! I soloed the thing. Shipley was my copilot. After we finished my period, I was copilot for him. It gives you a rather uneasy feeling to be sitting in there with someone soloing for the first time, but I wasn't scared.

I went over to the tailor shop to be measured for my uniform tonight. Reckon the day will ever come when I can wear it? I certainly hope so. I've done a whole lot of work not to get to. I'd sure be a disappointed fellow.

August 11, 22:15:

Things are rushing at me fast. I soloed yesterday and today I get my transition check. I rode with Capt. Hicks. He's a swell fellow, but I gave him a poor ride, as usual. I wrote Aunt Daisy a letter tonight. Levere's in California. We went on a cross-country run today, the back-woods road. Some of the guys saw their first raw cotton. They picked some of the stuff to bring back to the barracks.

August 12, 21:20:

I'm afraid I've got pilot's fatigue. In fact, everyone is moving around like a bunch of old men. Every movement seems to take a concentrated effort. I'd like to rest for about a month and just forget that I've ever seen an airplane. No, I suspect that's the wrong aspect. We've a war to win and, Rosey, you've got to do your part, so get busy and study for all four of those tests tomorrow.

I rode in the right seat in my dual ride today. I felt a little uneasy at first. I had another period in Link. I'm in radio work now. It is interesting and very important. I'm going to buckle down and learn the work.

No letter today. Oh! I think Betty and Mother have let me down. I think I'll still love them though.

August, Friday the thirteenth:

We were stationed at the Municipal Airport again today to shoot cross-wind landings. I didn't get to shoot any though. I acted as copilot for Saarela in the first period. We went down to Lake Park and landed a couple of times, then went back over to Municipal. We brought the plane back after we'd finished flying.

We had a rough day in ground school today. Had a test in instrument flying, navigation on the E6-B computer, Renshaw Aircraft Recognition, and a code check.

August 14, 22:00:

A little different type of day. Had a standby inspection this morning and a little close order drill. We were then dismissed for open post. I went over to the hospital to see Robinson, one of my buddies in the hospital, recovering from a hernia operation. I went down to visit Valdosta this evening with Sasser. We had a fairly good time, but my good times are limited until I can be with a certain person.

August 15, Sunday:

We flew this evening. I had a busy afternoon, divided between Link and flying. Sasser acted as my copilot today. I attended chapel this morning. We've got to fly in the morning. Yesterday was my little sister's birthday. She's twelve years old.

August 16, 21:30:

I'm dog-tired tonight. I flew all the periods today. I had dual crosswind landings at municipal and then I went up solo and then acted as copilot for Selch. I like to fly every period. It makes the day pass faster. We started new classes in ground school. Bombing and gunnery. We're taking naval recognition too. I'll declare all those ships look alike to me. Tony Pastor and his band are here tonight.

August 17, 20:40:

I don't think I'll ever get enough sleep again. I'd certainly like to try. We started flying instruments today

August 18, 19:10:

It's raining here. It's raining on the deep blue sea. Yes, sir! I mean we've had a small-scale flood this afternoon. The bad part is we missed calisthenics. Tsk tsk, too bad. I had another instrument ride this morning and rode as copilot for Sasser. He flew formation. It really looks hard. I'm supposed to start flying formation tomorrow.

August 19, 21:00:

Low ceiling this morning, no flying. I got in a period of Link and my *flight element visited the operations office. Lt. Delaney is really a swell fellow. We certainly like him. We went swimming with our clothes on in calisthenics today. I nearly froze.*

August 20, 21:00:

I had a bad day today. The first troublesome day in a long time. I don't know what causes it, but every little thing seems to irritate me. I got off to a bad start flying solo instruments, then I had to shoot ninety-degree stage at Municipal. Here's hoping I don't have anymore.

August 21, 20:00:

I had a rather easy day. I just had a period of Link and rode as copilot for three hours. We had our usual Saturday inspection. Barracks, personal, and a review. We are really lousy at marching. Getting worse by the day. No one seems to care though. I'm going to get some much-needed rest.

August 22, 21:30: Sunday!

And did I enjoy it. Slept through chapel this morning. I certainly hated to miss. My roommates stayed in over the weekend. We all got "sack" time. The only thing wrong with Sundays is that they pass too fast. I wish I could go home for about a year.

August 23, 22:45:

Off to another week. We are flying in the afternoons this week. I got my dual formation time in. I was off the ball. Lt. Delaney had to blow his top at me. I had to plot out all the cross-countries tonight. We have almost 2,500 miles of cross-country. I'll be glad to get started on them. I'm really sleepy. I've done a lot of work tonight.

August 24, 22:00:

Hey! They can't do this to me. I had another transition check. They've started back around for the second time. I rode with Capt. Hendel this time. He said it was a check to see how good our judgment was. We went around the traffic pattern twice.

August 25, 21:00:

I promised myself I would go to bed early tonight, but I won't be able to make it. One of my roommates, Saatela, went to the hospital yesterday with his ears. I sprained my ankle today in a "hard" game of volleyball. I don't know how I'll wake up in the morning. Saatela's our little alarm clock. Tomorrow's my birthday. I had a dog-fight with an AT-6. Me and Shipley again. I don't know whether we are in trouble again or not. I certainly hope not.

August 26, 22:00: Happy Birthday, Rosey!

You're twenty years old now, boy. Old age has just about got you. Well, here's wishing you many more, only under different circumstances, I hope. Truthfully, these last almost seven months have been the longest of any in my life. It's been pretty tough too, but I'm still alive and happy. I'm planning on being happier though. All they'd have to do is say the war's over and that I could go home. What a dream. Well, I'm ready to do my part to make this dream a reality. So, let's get busy, okay?

We went swimming with our pillowcases today. I busted mine wide open about the second time I went in. Lots of fun though.

August 27, 21:30:

We went on our first cross-country today. I rode with Lt. Delaney. We made the trip okay and then I rode as copilot and navigator for Yardley. We went to Pilmo, Yolee, Jasper, and returned. Yolee is just about twenty miles from the Atlantic coast, so we got lost a little and drifted out to the ocean. It was the first time I'd ever seen it. It certainly is a large drink of water.

August 28, 21:30: Graduation Day!

Yay for the upperclass. We've been busy all day. Practiced for the review this morning and had the review this afternoon. I carried the free French flag in the color guard group, which consisted of twenty-six flags representing the twenty-six nations. I just wish France was free. Just think, one month from today and I'm supposed to graduate. I can hardly wait.

I received a letter from Ralph Brown. He seems to be interested in Miss Francis Lowrance. Luck to the boy. I really like him. About the best pal a boy ever had.

August 29, Sunday:

This didn't seem so much like a Sunday. We flew this afternoon. Had an instrument cross-country. I flew by dead reckoning to McRea then flew the beam to Alma, then flew the beam back to Moody and made a low approach. Luckily, I came in over the field. My Link trainer was really disgusted this afternoon. I didn't even have to get in the Trainer.

August 30, 21:30:

Had another cross-country this morning. This was a low-altitude flight. We went to Jessup, Eastman, and returned. My copilot was Yardley. We didn't get so very low. I plotted out another cross-country. We never know when or which cross-country we'll have next. I'm the SOD tomorrow. Up until now, I've always escaped it. I'm the guide sergeant for Squadron H.

I'm going to try to go to bed. I hope I make it.

September 1, 21:00:

Whew! This SOD has just about knocked me out. The lower class, 43 J, came in yesterday evening and I know every one of them came to the office two or three times. I'm certainly glad it's over.

We took the final test in navigation this afternoon. We are going to take our physical examination test in PT tomorrow. I know I'll flunk it.

We are going to start night flying in a day or so. I'll be happy when night flying's finished. I don't care much for it. Believe me, it is lonesome.

September 2, 21:45:

We didn't get to fly much today. Had a low overcast. I finished my Link Trainer work today and got to fly an hour of dual formation. Lt. Delaney flew formation a little too close and clipped Shipley's horizontal stabilizer with our wing. About a foot of it crumpled like a piece of paper. Shipley didn't know it till he had landed and was back on the ramp.

September 3, 22:00:

We went on a high-altitude cross-country today. Newsome and I went to Statesboro, Milledgeville, and returned. It gets rather cool up there; I'd rather take low-altitude flights.

September 4, 21:30:

They must think I have a liking for high-altitude cross-countries. I went on another one today. We had our usual Saturday afternoon except we had a flight officer exam. It was rather farfetched I think. I like to drill for review better now since I'm practicing for my own graduation. I hope.

September 5, Sunday:

A peaceful day in "dear" old Georgia. I attended chapel this morning.

We're scheduled to fly tonight. I don't know how I feel about this night flying. In a way, I dread it, and this—I figure if anyone else can do it, I can do it.

September 6, 14:00:

Flying wasn't so bad last night. In fact, I enjoyed it. I rode with Lt. Bavinger. I really dreaded riding with him, but everything turned out okay. We shot floodlight and wing-light landings at Municipal. I had a solo ride the last period at Moody. H. R. Smith was my copilot. We didn't have breakfast until ten o'clock this morning. Swell life.

September 7, 15:00:

We had blitz landings last night. It was certainly black at Municipal. Too dark. I managed to find the ground okay though. I like night flying in this plane. I rode with Lt. Moses.

September 8, 15:30:

No flying last night. The fog was down next to the ground. Really grieved me. I would like to have flown. I'm eager to finish here. We fly this afternoon.

September 9, 21:30:

I went on another cross-country today. We had a strange field landing at Alma, Georgia. I was copilot for Musted. I'm not getting so much time in now. I've got an instrument check staring me in the face. Whew! I wish it was over and passed.

We finished ground school yesterday. That's one consolation. In place of ground school, we have maintenance engineering. I like to work on the plane. I'll bet they pull a double inspection after we're through working on though.

September 10, 22:00:

Had another morning of maintenance and went on the same cross-country that I took yesterday, only I went dual with Lt. Dolan. I'll get to rest a little tomorrow. No flying suits me fine.

September 11, 21:00:

We finished today's activities this morning at eleven o'clock. I've been getting some sack time. I got part of my uniform this evening.

September 12, 16:00:

Oh, boy! What a day. Rest and more rest. It turned rather chilly last night, just right for sleep and that's what I've been doing. I've written a few letters this afternoon. Just to think of having three more weeks and then graduation is enough to make me hilarious. We are flying tonight. I wonder what we'll do tomorrow afternoon. They'll have something though. We are going to shoot skeet two days next week.

September 13, 16:00:

We've started night cross-countries. Everyone's getting lost and having to ride the beam in. We ended up at Spence Field last night.

September 14, 16:30:

Flew again last night. I'll be glad when night flying is over. We got lost tonight and had to ride in on Alma beam and then the Moody beam. My, but that radio is a wonderful thing.

September 15, 15:30:

Last night of night flying this week. Two of my buddies, Ross and Selah, got lost last night and landed at Marianna, Florida. Capt. Hicks *was really mad today. He racked the whole squadron as soon as we arrived at the flight line and turned two chicken first lieutenants loose on us when we got inside. Oh, well! I'm just glad they didn't start the stuff sooner.*

September 16, 21:30:

We had to hit a brace again this morning. I had my instrument check with Capt. Hicks. He said there was nothing bad wrong, just a few minor details. I think they expect too much of a person. Squadron H put on an exhibition of functional swimming at the enlisted men's pool this afternoon. The water was really cold tonight. The main attraction was a group of bathing beauties (?) from some springs down in Florida. Ross Alle, the snake milker, gave a lecture and showed some reptiles.

September 17, 22:00:

I really had a swell afternoon skeet shooting. I was off the ball the first round but I managed to do pretty good the second round with fifteen birdies out of a possible twenty-five.

September 18, 21:30:

I had my time and distance interception cross-country. I arrived at the point of interception too early. I caught Capt. Horton as he came by though. We had an interesting talk by a major back from combat. He flew a B-24. I hope it gets one. Of course, we had our little room inspection, and believe it or not my roommate stood inspection with me. It was nice to have a little company for a change.

September 19, 15:00:

I'm always glad to see these Sundays roll around. They pass faster than any other day though. I attended chapel this morning. The weather seems to be rather low tonight. I don't know whether we'll get up or not.

September 20, 15:00:

Oh! Man, was I glad to get back on the ground last night. I went up as copilot for Starr. We went down to Municipal to shoot blitz landings. When we got there though, they wouldn't let us land. We flew in blinding rain until the clouds forced us down below the altitude of the traffic pattern, then the tower sent us back to Moody. After about an hour of circling and dodging red lights, we landed at the home field. Everyone turned a little gray. Today was Betty's birthday and I had forgotten all about it. Woe is me. I called her this morning though. I don't think she can come for graduation. I'd certainly love to see that sweet girl, and I'm not kidding.

September 21, 15:30:

The weather never did clear last night. I didn't care much, but I would love to finish night flying. I've just got a few hours cross-country and blitzes to make.

September 22:

I still didn't get any night flying. I had a solo instrument and a dual ride this afternoon. Lt. Delaney took me buzzing. We almost buzzed the bombing range. We flew a little formation with a couple of PT-17s. I think I took my last ride in the AF-10 at daytime. It doesn't make me unhappy in the least. No sirree. We were issued our wool and leather flying clothes this morning. We also were measured for our parachutes. It's going to be a big relief to fly in a parachute that fits. These GI things don't.

September 23, 15:00:

We've been getting a little extra sack time today. We are flying tonight and tomorrow night.

September 24, 14:00:

I've just come back from the subdepot. We went over to get my flying clothes and traveling bag. We are going to have a trainload of stuff to carry. I went on my dual cross-country last night. I rode with Lt. Sanders. I thought he was going to be tough but I enjoyed the ride. We went down to Gainesville, Florida, over to Dunnellon, back up to Cairo, and returned to Moody. It's a relief to get that dual ride over. I'd certainly hate to get lost with an instructor.

September 25, Saturday, 14:00:

Ah! My night flying is over and am I glad. I went on another cross-country and shot solo blitz landings, and what landings they were. Ten of them. These airplanes certainly take a beating. They must be tough.

Did I get a surprise today. We signed some papers over in cadet headquarters and I found out that I'm going to be second lieutenant. Whew! After two months of suspense. Really, I didn't know just what to expect, but I'm happy this p.m.

September 26, 20:00:

This has been a tiresome evening. We had to go to the flight line this afternoon. Just two or three flew though. All we had to do was kill time and it's killing me. If there's anything I hate to do it's to sit around on the flight line. We said good farewell to Lt. Delaney yesterday. He had a leave and left for his home in New York. He was a swell fellow. I'll be a long time forgetting him. I just hope I get a good instructor in transition.

September 27:

Same gruesome afternoon. Whew! But it takes a long time for an afternoon to pass. Am I disappointed. Betty called this morning and she isn't going to get to come to graduation. I'd better get a leave. I'll bet they are wonderful things. Shipley and I drove the line taxi this afternoon.

September 28, 22:00:

We were released from the flight line today. It's beginning to look as if I might finish here. That will be a happy day. I had my logbook certified this afternoon. I've got over two hundred hours of pilot time now. I had a stencil cut with my new serial number: O813783. That Lt. in front of my name looks big to me. Yes, sir, I'm glad to see that. No fooling.

September 29, 21:30:

I went over after my parachute this morning. It's one of the new nylon instead of the silk jobs. I suspect I'll be hitting the nylon instead of the silk. Anyway, I'm glad to have my own chute. I've turned in my ground school supplies. Am I anxious to get through. I'm not going to be an instructor. They've talked to the future instructors. I've had a dread of being an instructor all the way through.

September 30, 23:00:

We've been milling around all day, packing, talking about a furlough and etc. I'm having a tough time getting my stuff together. I had my picture made in my leather flying clothes this morning. We've had to wear our gas masks all day. They had tear gas attacks. I've just come back from the graduation dance. It was just getting started.

Tomorrow's the day. After eight months of hard work and sweating, I'm about to graduate. I hope I can go to sleep tonight.

October 1, 15:00:

I've done it. We've received our commission this morning down on the drill field and then marched over to the post theater and were given our wings. I got my orders a few minutes ago and I'm to report to Sebring, Florida, on October 13, to fly Fortresses. Home and leave. Someone wake me up!

Pilot and Officer

October 13, 1943, 21:00:

I am now a second lieutenant in the Army Air Forces. Graduating from twin-engine advanced school at Moody Field, Valdosta, Georgia, October 1, 1943. The few days since October 1 have been spent with my parents at their new home in Harriman, Tennessee.

The time was shortened by the presence of a most wonderful visitor. Yep, you guessed it. Miss Betty Thomas from LaFayette, Georgia. I have never known time to fly so fast.

This book is a graduation present from my aunt Jane Pope. Thank you, Aunt Jane. While on my leave we visited our hometown of Chattanooga three times. It was there I caught the train last Tuesday, the twelfth, for Sebring, Florida, to fly B-17s, or Flying Fortresses.

I arrived downtown this afternoon at about 15:50 hours and, to my disappointment, my baggage failed to arrive. That would not have been so bad but my special orders were in the suitcase. I came on out to the field, signed in at the front gate at 16:17 hours, accompanied by a buddy from Moody, C. R. Mitchell. We proceeded to personnel head-quarters and signed in okay. I used one of his orders and got through all of the stuff. I promised to take some of my papers over when they came, but I don't suspect there's any use in it.

I've two new roommates. Roth from Tampa, Florida, and Roeder from New York. I believe I'll like this field fine. Everything's agreeable so far. I was really homesick coming down on the train and I still have a little tinge of it left. Kinda lonesome, huh?

October 14, Thursday, 21:03:

What a life. I slept until eight o'clock, got breakfast, got my baggage out of supply, straightened up a little, ate dinner, and then marched over to the post theater. We had orientation lectures from three or four officers, post commander, commandant of students, chaplain, and from the flight surgeon. After the lectures, we went to the flight line and met our instructors and squadron commanders, and etc.

Then we were officially introduced to the B-17E. After ramming my head, skinning my knees, and, in general, bruising my whole body, I managed to get to the pilot's compartment. There, I was greeted by a thousand and one new gadgets. We were shown this and that for about an hour then went back into the flight office and talked a while.

My new instructor is Lt. Abraham. He's a small fellow, but seems to be agreeable and easy to get along with. Let's all hope so, okay? After listening to all the little speeches today, I'm sure our stay here isn't going to be an easy one, but I think I'm going to enjoy it. I'm supposed to go up tomorrow.

October 15, Friday, 21:30:

Oh, boy, what an airplane. I'm really going to like this thing. The instructor and three of us students went up this morning. We flew around a little while, feathered a prop, done stall approach, then we went up to Brooksville airport, about one hundred miles distance north of Tampa, to shoot some landings. The instructor shot about six landings and then let us land three times apiece. I was the last student so I got to fly back to the home field. The other Fortresses joined us in formation and we led in a six-ship formation.

It's really a dream to land. Only thing is it takes all the pull there is in a person to hold back on the stick. The thing that awed me the most was the use of the trim tabs which we didn't use. The thing flies without using them. I rode in the bombardier's nose a little while—that's great fun. We had PT this afternoon.

October 18, Monday:

I've been wearing a different type of uniform since Saturday. It's in the form of pajamas. Yup, you guessed it, I'm in the hospital, or rather, I was in the hospital. I was fully released this morning.

It all happened Saturday morning around 10:30 while I was taking physical training. I was participating in a little harmless basketball and I jumped up to catch a rebound from the backboard. Well, I ended up in a three-point position, flat on my fanny for a few minutes. I didn't know which was broken, my hand or my rear end. X-rays later proved, though, that it was my hand.

Somehow, I pulled myself up and walked over to see the PT instructor. He sent me to the first-aid barracks. The first-aid man sent me to the flight surgeon. The flight surgeon sent me to the X-ray department. X-ray sent me back to the flight surgeon. The flight surgeon sent me to the sick and wounded office. They took me to ward four, where they bathed me a little and issued me a pair of pajamas, robe, and house shoes. After about four hours of waiting, they wheeled me down to the operating room in a wheelchair.

Truthfully, I've never felt so helpless in my life. They wouldn't hear of me walking. Here's hoping I never have to ride one of those things again.

Major West splinted my arm up okay. I had a fractured radius bone in my wrist. "Pop" Chute wheeled me back to my room. I had a private room and bath, food served to me in bed. Really, it was a life of ease. However, I've never been so glad to be out of a place in all my life. I like to have never gone to sleep. Saturday, around twelve o'clock, I called the ward boy and he got the nurse to fix me some sleeping capsules. It wasn't long until I was in slumber heaven. I laid around all day Sunday. Such a long day I've never seen. I had little trouble going to sleep last night though, for which I am very thankful.

I talked to the flight surgeon this morning and he talked like he would send me home. Oh, boy! I certainly would love that. It's really hurting me about losing my class though. I didn't know I loved flying so much until I got hurt and now I can't fly. Major West said it would be a month longer before I would fly again. These big babies do something to me when they roar over for a landing, I'm telling you.

Oh well, it's a lot of rough luck. I worried a lot Saturday night, but I've just about decided that everything might work out for the best. Anyway, here's hoping I get to go home.

November 5, 13:00:

I'm just off from duty as JSOD. I went on yesterday to relieve an upperclassman so he could attend the dance last night. I haven't ridden a bicycle so much in a long time. I know a place that's going to be sore, and I'm not kidding

I was on duty at the graduation dance, and did I have a time. I just had to take one fellow home though. They were all on the verge. I was chased by one girl most of the night. She kept chasing me try-ing to make me take a drink. She said I had taken her husband's place as JSOD and they wanted to give me a drink. They finally quit pestering me.

I'm just a little sleepy this afternoon. I noticed the last time I wrote in this diary that I was talking about going home. I've long ago given up the idea. I'm assigned to the 453rd training squadron as asst. engineering officer. I've been in the inspection dept. the last two weeks. I have a swell bunch of boys and I enjoy working with them. They are T/Sgt. Jenks, T/Sgt. Wrable, S/Sgt. Moran, S/Sgt. Johnson, S/Sgt. Christsen, Cpl. Goerl, Cpl. Smith, and Cpl. Yojmack. T/Sgt. Wrable has been transferred to combat duty now. Best of luck to him. I wish I was ready to go. I've had a few blue moments since my wrist has been broken. I wish I could express my feelings of helplessness. Something in me wants to go on training and just the thought of being held back is enough to make me cry, almost. I have a pretty good time though. I suspect I can't complain.

I called that sweet Betty this afternoon. She told me some wonderful news. If you'd like to know what it was, ask her. She's a wonderful girl.

November 11, Armistice Day, Thursday 21:00:

If only history could repeat itself today. My, would that be too good to be true. I can just see myself going home to stay. Come back to Earth,

Rosey. Not getting to go home with this broken arm makes me feel like the WAC that went out to get a snack and came back with a tidbit. I'm not so disappointed though, and I'm still almost as eager and deter-mined as the little moron that killed his parents so he could attend the orphan's picnic. This is one glorious life.

I went for a ride in the B-17 last night with Sasser and Schomp. We went back up over Moody Field. We got lost coming back and found ourselves over at Tampa. I'll be a happy boy when I start flying again.

November 17, 22:00:

I'm just about back in the saddle again. I'm almost a well boy now. I took the little splint off my arm last Friday night. My arm is gaining strength rapidly. I was put back on flying status yesterday. No more DNIF staff for me. I hope, hope, hope I'm over in my new quarters to-night. I'm to fly with the new class of 43-3, the same class I started with back at Maxwell, so I'm back where I started from.

I hate to lose all my buddies. I don't know a living soul in this whole barrack. I haven't stayed here but a few minutes though. I played basketball awhile this afternoon and watched them play to-night. We're going to enter a student officers team in the league I think. It's rather lonesome in this room by myself. It's good to be back in training again though. I'm in the 451st Squadron Flt C. We're to fly tomorrow afternoon.

November 18:

Off to the first day of training. I got up a little earlier this morning than usual. I've been staying in bed every morning until 08:30. I'll have to get up on the ball now though.

We're to have court-martial this morning in ground school and fly-ing this afternoon. Make this first day a good one, Rosey.

November 19, 08:30:

I can't stand much of this getting up early stuff. I'd rather sleep until up in the morning. I see now that I didn't appreciate my soft job down at the 453rd. I went down hoping to fly yesterday afternoon and I had maintenance instead. Did I feel let down after having a solid month of nothing but maintenance. Oh well, maybe I'll start this morning. I hope not though, because I banged up my right thumb playing basketball yesterday afternoon.

I have more troubles. I talked to Capt. Harris last night.

21:30: *Another day and still no flying. I'm not getting impatient though. I've waited a month, a few days don't mean anything. Rolled out of bed at 05:15 this morning. I'm going to start going to bed earlier. I had maintenance again this morning. Rudow and I went down to 453rd to see the boys. Cpl. Yonack has bet me five dollars that I'll be a captain by February 1945. That's a long time off. I hope the war is over and I'm home by then. In fact, I wouldn't care if the war was over now.*

I tried to mail Dabber some candy this afternoon but I didn't have a letter from him requesting it, so I called. Couldn't get through. He's over in Italy raising Hell with the enemy. I wish I was over there helping him. I just have five more months before I can go. It's certainly a long time to train. I like it though.

November 20, 21:00:

At last! Believe it or not but I flew an airplane this afternoon. I'm just a little tired tonight. The B-17 is a handful to fly but do I love it. My captain, Baird, is a strictly swell fellow. I'm really lucky to have a good instructor like him. He's the flight commander, and can he fly that airplane.

I witnessed a crash landing today. It's a sickening sight to see that crippled thing coming down knowing that it will be ruined. This is too good of an airplane to be landing on the belly. The drag link in one of the landing gear assemblies was broken. He came in with one of the wheels dangling. That's the fourth airplane to do that since I've been here. I'm glad Mother doesn't know about these things. She wouldn't let me fly anymore. Yeh!

November 21, 18:15:

We flew again this morning. I'm going to be getting flying pay. Now isn't that something. It comes in handy though and no income tax to pay on it either.

Flight C had a little mix-up on their schedule this morning. The daily bulletin read that we would fly this afternoon but the instructors said this morning. Well, we went by the bulletin board and stayed in the sack this morning.

About 06:15 hours I was awakened by the slamming of doors and the bellowing of a couple of officers. Were they hot and did they wake everyone up. One of them happened to be my instructor. The other two fellows in my element, Sproul and Tell, were in Lakeland, Florida. They thought we were flying this afternoon. Capt. Baird took us duck hunting on Lake Okeechobee this morning. Some fun.

November 22, 20:00:

I had some good experience this morning. We had been going around the traffic pattern for about half an hour, I had just settled in the pilot's seat when Capt. Baird said, "Look at that." He was working the No. 1 throttle to its limits but the manifold pressure failed to respond. So he feathered the prop. He asked me if I wanted to make a three-engine approach. Of course I did; it really wasn't difficult or hard, but knowing that one engine was gone was a sensation that I don't know how to express. That motionless prop certainly isn't a heartwarming sight. However, it isn't anything to worry about.

I got an hour of maintenance unfeathering the prop and spent the rest of the morning in cockpit drill.

I had thirteen boys out for basketball practice this afternoon. Very encouraging.

November 24, 21:30:

I flew last night and this afternoon. We went on a navigation flight last night around the horn, or maybe I'd better say the state of Florida so you'll know where I mean. Yep, the dear old state of Florida. They can give it back to the Indians as far as I'm concerned. I've always heard of the beauty of this state but so far I've never seen any of that famed beauty. Maybe I've had my eyes closed. It's all swamp to me.

We had an instrument navigation flight this afternoon. We went to Tampa, Gross City, Orlando, Melbourne, West Palm Beach, Miami, and return.

Capt. really got p-ed off at me for not knowing how to work the loop. I don't know what he expects. He made us crank the wheels when we came back to the field. I don't know whether he's going to smile or chew me (smile, I hope).

November 25, 23:00, 1943, Thanksgiving Day:

What a day! What a dinner! Here's the menu: Shrimp cocktail, turkey noodle soup, roast turkey with oyster dressing, stuffing-mashed potato, giblet gravy, cranberry sauce, corn on the cob, buttered English peas, tomato and lettuce salad with mayonnaise, hot rolls and butter, minced-apple pie, pumpkin pie, fresh apples, grapes, oranges, bananas, assorted hard candies, assorted nuts, ice cream, radishes, assorted pickles, olives, celery, iced tea with lemon, and coffee and cream.

I'm going to send the menu to Mother to show her how poorly they feed in the army. I'd rather be home eating her cooking than anything I've ever eaten in the army. I'm not kidding, she really knows how to do that stuff called cooking. Most everyone on the field had the day off.

November 26, 18:00:

I've gone to ground school all day. I like ground school here okay. It's the real stuff. They really dish it out. They have to though there's so much to learn and such a short time to learn it in. I'm working hard to absorb all of it I can. I know it'll make the difference between me coming back or not coming back someday. Personally, I prefer coming back. There's a lot of good people I'd like to see after the war. I think I'll spend the first year after the war doing nothing but enjoying life. What a life that will be. Imagine going to bed and getting up when you please. You'd better imagine. Right now I'm busy winning a war.

November 27, 22:00:

I flew the Link last night; that wasn't so bad, but when I went down to fly this afternoon, I had to fly the Link again. In two trips, I have five and a half hours. That's more time than I flew the whole nine weeks in primary.

They have some WAC instructors in the Links. I hope I never get one. It's enough worry to fly the thing let alone a little squeaky-voiced girl out there yelling at you. I prefer a male instructor.

I've just returned from a basketball game. It was our first game of the season. Of course, we were beaten. We don't feel bad though. In fact, I think we did exceptionally well. In the first place, we played the champions of last year's tournament. I introduced one half of our team to the other half just a few minutes before the game. I believe we could have beaten them with a little practice.

November 28, Sunday, 22:00:

This has been a beautiful day. I had maintenance this morning. In contrast to most maintenance periods, I learned a little this morning. I went back down to the 453rd and subdepot. One of the electricians took my friend, Tell, and me through the electric shops and explained and demonstrated a lot of stuff to us. Then we went back out to some of the planes and he pointed out several different things. We certainly appreciated his help and interest. I think his name is Scholsberg.

I missed going to chapel this morning. The Chaplains here are the best I've had since coming into the army. Both of them are from Tennessee. Chaplain Horldt from Chattanooga and Chaplain Hastings from Memphis.

November 29, Monday, 12:55:

It's raining here, whew! I'm telling you, it's a regular Florida outpour. I'm going to ground school this morning. We had approach. They had the very secret bomb sight out. Just a few months ago, it had to be guarded with dear life. Now it is only confidential. The Germans had too many of them.

23:30: *My instructor took a rest tonight and gave us maintenance. We were supposed to have stayed on the line until twelve tonight, but he left and so did we. We watched a little of a ball game tonight and went back to sign in our time. I hope Capt. Baird doesn't catch us. He would really work on our ding-dong and I'm not kidding.*

We had a little cross-country run in PT this afternoon.

November 30, 22:00:

Payday today. Yep, today was the big day of the month. Did I have an afternoon. We had two- and three-engine landings and three-engine takeoffs. A fellow needs a kick like a mule wears to boot those rudders around. I received a lot of valuable information today. I hope I never need to use it though. I think I'd like four good engines to run on. Doesn't fly any too well on three engines, not to speak of just having two. I'm going to take good care of my plane when it's issued.

I've never felt so sorry for anyone in my life as I did Sproul today.

I mean the captain really ate him a new one. Sproul deserved it though.

The 453rd beat us in basketball tonight.

December 1, 23:00:

Higher, higher, and higher we fly. I had my first real altitude flight this morning. There was nothing to it. We just put on our heavy equipment and climbed up to twenty thousand feet. It was a little chilly up there, but most of the time, I was sweating.

We met four other ships over Lake Okeechobee and flew formation. One of the engines on one of the ships caught fire and had to return to the field. Upon landing, its prop and front part of the engine flew off.

I was in a hot sweat when we finally got down. We finished up the morning with hooded takeoffs. They aren't so hard. In fact, they were comparatively simple. I love to fly this airplane.

December 6, 22:00:

Am I a proud lad tonight, yes, sir! I soloed this big monster today. Tell and I flew together. We flew instruments most of the afternoon. Truthfully, I believe this is the easiest and safest airplane in the world to fly. I thought for a while that I would like to go to B-29s but I've changed my mind. I'll stick with this old girl. Capt. Baird certainly gets hot under the collar easily. We like him okay though.

December 7, 1943:

Two years after Pearl Harbor. The story has changed a little since then though. Those rotten little fellows haven't been beat yet, but just wait.

December 13, 21:30:

I know I'm the tiredest boy in this part of the world. We left this *morning around two o'clock for Memphis. I slept about an hour last night before I left. We flew all morning and most of the afternoon. We left Memphis around twelve noon. The trip going up was okay. We passed over Chattanooga this morning at daybreak. I've never seen such a wonderful sunrise. It looked good to an old homesick boy. My, but I'd love to be home, but not until after the war.*

We ended up at Pensacola, Florida, on the trip back. We were just about one hundred miles off course. Captain really raged. Maybe he'll get over it though. Here's hope for no more long cross-countries.

December 19, Sunday, 15:50:

I've never known time to pass so fast in all my life. The last two or three weeks have slipped by like so much greased lightning. If the remainder of the time here passes as fast, I'll be leaving tomorrow or the next day.

At present, I have seventy-five hours in the Fortress. We finished formation and altitude work this morning. I didn't get to attend chapel this morning.

I rode with Capt. Williams of the Standardization Board yesterday. He was giving me a workout, only the tower called us to go to Knoxville to get some passengers. There were three officers and one WAC officer to come back. Need I say more? Sasser is spending the night with me.

December 24, 16:00:

'Twas the night before Christmas, when all through the post, not a GI was stirring, they all left camp. Yep, this is the loneliest Yule I ever hope to spend. I had planned on meeting my grandmother, uncle Audie, and family at Boynton Beach, but I have been unable to contact them by phone. I had a letter from Mother saying that they were moving back to Tennessee in a few days so I suspect they've already left the wilderness of Florida. I would have liked to have seen them though. In fact, I'd like to see anyone.

I'll bet if Betty knew who I was having dinner with tonight she would shoot me. I'm having dinner with a female corporal. You guessed it, a WAC. Jeanne, from North Carolina. I met her about six weeks ago at the Supply. I like her and enjoy talking with her.

Of course, there could be no one else but Betty. She means everything to me. What I wouldn't give to see her tonight. My family sent me the most beautiful watch. I love all of them.

December 28, 21:30:

What a day! We went up this morning for bomb approach work. The fog was right on the ground. We couldn't even see the end of the runway we were taking off on. We started off by using Sebring as a target but it was so fogged in we could hardly see it so we ended up using Hendricks Field. I got a big kick out of Walters; he said he was bombing the Mess Hall. I couldn't have cared if he demolished it. A replacement would have had to be an improvement.

We were just getting off to a good start when the tower called us in to form a search mission. One of the ships was missing from last night. When we landed, there was only one runway clear of fog. We waited around until eleven o'clock and were just about to leave when one of the ships called in and reported the ship to be about four hundred yards off of runway thirteen. No one knows when or just what caused the accident. The fog was on the ground so I suspect he was attempting to hit the field on instruments maybe. I'll find out in a day or so. The plane was a total loss and so were the mangled bodies of five good men.

The sole topic of conversation in the field is the crash. I hope to goodness my folks don't read about it in the paper. Of all the flying done, there are bound to be a few accidents. There's been about five crash landings since I've been here. No one ever gets hurt though. The last night we flew, five of the airplanes came in with one engine gone. I still think this is the safest airplane. I really like it. It's the only airplane I've felt like I could fly.

January 1, 1944, New Year's Day:
Off to another fresh year, one which I am sure will be the most out-standing year of my life. One in which the war will end or one in which I will see the war. Personally, I'm not afraid of war, in fact, I rather look forward to it, but I'd rather go home than any place I know of. I'm sick of the army. I'm tired of the routine life, the same old thing day in and day out.

I'm not bitching though; I'll be in here till the last one's gone and still get along fine. I'm about to wind every little thing up here. We're finishing fast, just a few more flights and a little more ground school, and then off to operational training.

Here's wishing the good old USA the best and victory in 1944. Rosey's going to be in there pitching.

January 6, 14:10:
Am I a disgusted individual. Do I know a bunch of boys that will be a long time forgetting a certain Col. Higgins, CO of Hendricks Field.

Up to the last class, all the students have been finishing early and getting a leave. But along comes dear Col. Higgins and puts a stop to the whole affair. My flight is ahead of the whole field in flying time, so the colonel grounds us to slow us down. Instead of flying, we get maintenance. Do we love that old chap. It takes a man with no heart to cheat us out of our leaves. I don't know whether he thinks of it or not, but this will probably be our last opportunity of going home before go-ing overseas. Oh, well! War'll be over in six or seven years. Why worry? Best of regards to you, Col. Higgins.

January 15, 21:00:
I certainly hope this isn't getting to be a habit, but Hendricks Field had another fatal airplane crash. This one happened at Ft. Worth, Texas. The two boys across the hall, Thoman and Stiles, saw the thing go down to its finish.

It was approaching the field in a normal approach. They noticed *some smoke pouring out of one of the engines. The airplane then went up into a partial lazy eight and kept going into the ground on one wing. Nothing to speak of was left of the ship. It exploded when it struck the ground. I wish these accidents would cease. That's ten more good men gone. A total of sixteen men in about two weeks. If a few more get killed, they should give us campaign ribbons for going through Hendricks Field.*

I flew bomb approach with Inst. Lt. Barker this afternoon. PDI and I mean plenty of it. I don't like Barker's personality as an instructor. He has the air of a major with a 1st Lt. bar.

I've been thinking of Betty a lot.

January 19, 17:00:

It won't be long now. Yep, I'll be leaving Hendricks Field in a matter of hours. I cleared most of the field yesterday. All we had to do today was to clear operations, laundry, and SO supply. We received our shipping orders this morning. I'm going to Plant Park, Tampa, Florida. It's a replacement depot for the Third Air Force. No one seems to know a thing about it. I'll find out in a day or so though.

I'm going over to say farewell to Jane Harris tonight. I've learned to like her these last few weeks. I think she's a strictly swell girl. I'll spend the night in town and go to Tampa in the morning. Most of the boys have already taken off. I hate to leave this field. I like it better than any other where I've been stationed. Well, here's a fond farewell to Hendricks Field and hoping I'll come back to it someday.

January 20, 20:00: Plant Park, Tampa, Florida

I arrived in Tampa about 1400 hours this afternoon. I came up on the bus with Rodow, one of my roommates at Maxwell Field. We ate lunch in town and then came on out here to this place. I spent the night in the "Blue Room" of the Clair Hotel in Sebring. My roommate was Charles A. White. Charlie fell in love with one of the WACs at Hendricks. She's Pat Shelton, a cute thing too. Charlie's going to Clovis, New Mexico, to be a copilot on the new B-29.

Now, about this hole where I'm stationed. I've never been in a place like this before. Nashville was Heaven as compared to this place. We are living in tents. There are four of us in this one. Our combined rent for this tent will be $180. Rather high for a tent?

Besides being a hole to live in, we know nothing of what we'll be doing here. We don't know how long we'll be here or nothing at all. All I can say is that I signed in, saw the adjutant, went through plans and routing, reported to detachment, was assigned a tent, and here I am, well and contented.

I have an appointment with the flight surgeon tomorrow at 1300 hours. I have two blankets to keep me warm tonight. It's so chilly here that I'll need four blankets. Here's hoping I don't freeze. Let's go see the town of Tampa. I know one place I'd like to be tonight. I certainly hope our stay here will be as short as possible. I'm ready to leave now.

January 21, 18:00:

Can they do this to us? The first thing they did to us was to give us a mass close-order drill in practice for a parade tomorrow. I nearly froze last night. I couldn't sleep. The last two hours this morning, my feet were two chunks of ice. Cob this stuff.

I went through classification this afternoon. What a tiring affair. I received those pleasant shots this afternoon. The big football-like fellow shot me with that little needle so fast I didn't know what was happening.

I met a girl last night that looked just like Betty. It really made me lonesome and did I miss Betty. The girl's name is Barbara Sosa. She is a Spanish girl. I'm finding out about tent city. The ballpark here is the training home of the Cincinnati Reds. They can give my part of that field to the Reds.

January 24, 18:00:

We're still running to and fro here. I went to a high-altitude lecture this morning and then to the chamber at MacDill Field this afternoon.

There were twelve of us in that little chamber. We went up to twenty thousand feet and stayed there for ten minutes before putting on our mask. I thought I would pass out but I stuck it out and made it okay. We went on up to twenty-eight thousand feet and leveled off. One of the boys went all the way up to twenty-eight thousand feet without oxygen. They let him keep off his mask until he was ready to pass out. It was amusing to see him try to write the ABCs. He had a hard time adding 4 + 4. The truck left us and we had to get a ride back or stay until 2030 hours for the truck to get back. I caught a ride with a T/Sgt.

January 25, 20:00:

Well, was I in for a surprise this morning. I'm on the alert list for immediate shipment. Suits me okay. Of all things, I'm going to Avon Park Field about fifteen miles from Hendricks. Several of my classmates are stationed there. I don't know when we will leave yet—soon, I hope. I think it will be Thursday the twenty-seventh.

My ears have been popping all day. I don't think that twenty-eight thousand feet hop did them any good last night. I went to St. Petersburg, Florida, last night with Wm. M. Wood, one of the boys from Hendricks. I'll never forget what I did last night. I never planned on it, never. Oh well, it really wasn't that bad though.

Well, here's for Avon Park and wishing for me the best there. I'm staying in and writing letters tonight.

January 29, 08:00:

We got another surprise: I'm not going to Avon Park. They've changed the orders. I'm being sent to Drew Field here in Tampa. I'm in a pickle. I've had my mail sent to Avon Park. Some of the boys have even sent their baggage and wives down. Oh, well, just another army fuddle. I was hoping to go to Avon Park. I'd like to get back to the wilderness again. I didn't know I liked the place so well.

I suppose I can make out at Drew. Here's hoping anyway. I met my copilot. His name is Humbert Lucketti from Easton, Pennsylvania.

Truthfully, if the rest of the crew suits me as well as he does, I know we'll have a good crew. Here's to you and me, Lucketti. We are leaving for Drew Field at about 1300 hours this afternoon. I suspect I'd better start packing. So long, Plant Park, and all you tents.

January 30, 11:30: Sunday morning, Drew Field, Tampa

We arrived here yesterday afternoon at about 1500 hours by GI truck from Plant Park. I must say, we're in for walking and more walking. This field is spread out over an area of ten miles. We live on the south side and must meet all formations on the north side. Yes, good management. Just like everywhere else.

The barracks here are okay. I'm rooming with my copilot, Lucketti. The mess and mess hall are okay. In fact, it's good. We eat cafeteria-style at fifty cents a meal. Not nearly as bad as I expected.

I have just returned from a hurried G9 examination. I was greeted by a GI coming out the door with one of those needles. They couldn't even wait until we were inside. I had a shot outside and two more when I got inside. I have a few more then I'll be finished, or perforated one.

January 31, 19:30:

At last, the day I've been looking forward to. I met my crew this morning and am I pleased. Yep, they all seem like a good bunch of boys. I'll start with my bombardier, Bertrand Morin from Maine. He's the oldest crew member. Seems to be serious, on the ball, type. Works on crossword puzzles continuously.

My aerial engineer is Gasgue, Lacy F., a sergeant from Alabama. He's a typical 'bama boy. A little heavy, full-faced, freckled with light brown hair.

Asst. aerial engineer is Sgt. Donnan R. Smeallie. Smeallie just got married a week ago; I suspect I'll have to take it easy on him. Best of luck, Smeallie.

Radio operator is Herman R. Riep from Idaho. He's a dark-skinned frank, honest-looking type.

Asst. Radio operator Pfc. Major A. Burnett. I don't know what to say of Burnett. He seems to have a good personality, wants to learn radio too. Riep and Burnett are old cadets that washed out.

Armorer is Cpl. Wm. M. Smith. Smith is married, from Ohio, and seems to be the lively one of the crew.

Asst. armorer and tail gunner is Cpl. George W. Ivey from Georgia. Ivey is the quietest one on the whole crew. He'll come around though. The entire crew is nice-looking boys. I can't say much about Lucketti. He'll read it here. He's strictly okay with a few ideas.

February 2, 22:00:

I'm looking for trouble now. I went to town and brought out my monkey, Turbo. He is really a mess. It is going to cost to get him cleaned up after. He is really popular. Ten or twelve boys are playing with him constantly. Here's hoping we make it out together.

February 4:

First anniversary in the army. One year ago today, I was really a sad sack. Yep, there in Nashville, Tennessee, not knowing what was in store for me, away from home, and wanting to go back to see my mother.

I'm still a sad sack but I've learned a little since then. I've had eight months of cadet training and four months of training as an officer. I have a total of 350 hours of pilot time. However, I still want to go home to see my mother. Someone else I'd like to see too, meaning you, Betty.

February 6, Sunday, 22:00:

We were supposed to have flown last night but there weren't enough planes for the entire flight, so Rosey and his boys sat on their flat backends and had a two-hour bull session. It was interesting to talk to the boys. We had a discussion of gunnery, etc.

I went back to Hendricks Field yesterday afternoon and came back this morning. I saw several of my old friends. I talked to Jeanne last night. She's okay.

Sunday is just another day on the field. We go to ground school on Sunday the same as any other day. We have a tiring schedule for four days then we have the fifth day off. Not bad but I think we should have Sunday off, don't you? Let's get some much-needed sleep. We get up at 0300 hours when we fly in the morning, at 0500 hours to go to ground school. Rather early, no?

February 8, 21:00:

Well, well, we did get to fly. After about two hours of briefing, we got off this morning. I rode with instructor pilot Lt. Bowley. We went on a search mission for some boys that have been in the sea for about five days. They were from the field. They picked up one raft with four of the fellows. The other raft is still out there. We flew in a three-ship formation about three hundred to four hundred feet off the water; it was really awesome.

After about three hours, we returned to the field. We shot two landings, Lt. Bowley got out and let us go up. I don't know yet what Lucky thinks about the plane. I think he's convinced that he has more to do than ride in the right seat. I suspect I got too irritated today.

BETTY AND GRADY
AND A WEDDING

In January, Grady wrote Betty that he felt they should "go ahead" and get married. Betty and Grady had discussed marriage since it became clear that Grady was going into service. She told me it was always something he was in favor of and, without admitting as much, that she was the voice of reason and patience. The true reasons are more involved and complicated than understood than we know now, but Betty agreed and the marriage process started.

Betty was too young to marry without consent and cooperation from her father, Carlos. That required State of Georgia paperwork. Betty told me, "He was not thrilled but he agreed, and we went to LaFayette where he signed for me." Next, a date of February 22, 1944, was set and Grady was to arrange things at Drew Field, Florida.

Betty's best friend in LaFayette was Violet Hawkins. When Betty told Violet of her plans to go to Tampa, Florida, and get married, Violet was upset by the idea that Betty would ride a bus to Tampa by herself. She insisted that she and her sister Ruby should go along.

Betty "enjoyed" her work at the Walker County Welfare Department and the department was pleased with her job performance and suggested that if she "would catch up the work which accumulated while she was away" she could go to Florida with their blessing.

Early Monday morning, February 21, 1944, Betty, with Violet and Ruby, boarded a bus in LaFayette and headed to Tampa, Florida. Her luggage for the trip and the unknown time she would be spending in Tampa as a newlywed was a medium-sized suitcase containing her "personal things and a couple of changes of clothes." The trio rode all night and got into Tampa around ten o'clock Tuesday morning, the twenty-second of February. The planning director of the wedding had failed to consider the business closures due to Washington's birthday observance. The courthouse was closed on February 22 in honor of Washington, so the final paperwork could not be processed.

Betty, Violet, and Ruby got a room at the Floridan Palace Hotel which was close to the courthouse, bus station, a seafood restaurant, and a movie theater. Grady met them and, after a meal at the seafood restaurant, they all went to the movie theater and watched *White Christmas*. After the movie, Grady went back to the base and the girls went to the hotel and "waited."

The wedding was scheduled for ten o'clock the next morning. A friend of Grady's had a car and offered Grady the use of his car to make things easier for the wedding process. When Grady went by to pick up the car, his friend "was nowhere to be found." Grady took the bus to town, they got all the paperwork done, and then took the bus back to the base. All turned out well, as they had a high noon wedding in the chapel at Drew Field Air Force Base.

The Chattanooga newspaper announced the wedding like this:

> *Rozzell-Thomas Bridal in Tampa*
> *Groom Chattanoogan, Bride from LaFayette, GA, the wedding of Miss Betty Caroline Thomas and Lt W. G. Rozzell of Chattanooga and Tampa, Florida, took place February 23 at high noon at the Post Chapel, Drew Field Tampa. Maj Carl W. Hewlett, Chaplain officiated and a small entourage of close friends were present.*

> The bride's attendant was Miss Violet Hawkins of LaFayette, maiden of honor, and Lt. Humbret Lucketti of Drew Field was best man.
>
> The bride wore an ashes of roses crepe two-piece dress with black pumps and a corsage of white. The maiden of honor wore a powder blue suit and her flowers were Talisman roses.
>
> The bride is the only daughter of Mr. and Mrs. C. D. Thomas of LaFayette and a sister of Joel Thomas of Trion, GA. She is a graduate of LaFayette High School and Edmonson School of Business in Chattanooga and the past year has held a secretarial position with the Walker County Dept of Public Works
>
> The bridegroom is the only son of Mr. and Mrs. D.F. Rozzell and his sister is Miss Nancy Rozzell.
>
> He is a graduate of Central High School and attended the University of Chattanooga when he entered the Army Air Corp. The couple will reside in Tampa.
>
> Miss Ruby Hawkins was among those attending the reception.

The newspaper did not report the dress of the bridegroom but Betty was not shy in detailing the uniform and attitude as "nothing is more handsome than an arrogant 2nd Lt. wearing silver wings and pinks and greens. That is what Grady wore to our wedding."

After the ceremony, the wedding party, minus Lt. Lucketti, rode the bus back to town. They ate lunch at the seafood restaurant. Violet and Ruby Hawkins took the three o'clock coach back to LaFayette. Betty and Grady were without a residence so they settled into the Floridan while Betty searched for a place to live.

Tampa was a military town at the time and most of the residents were friendly to the situation of servicemen and women like the new Mr. and Mrs. Rozzell. Betty talked to a few of the volunteer agencies which existed to help young couples and she looked at "many fleabag rooms" before she found a nice room with bathroom privileges. The room she took was at 828 S. Rome Avenue. It was on the streetcar line and was only five blocks from the bay and she walked there often. They had no kitchen privileges but neither ate breakfast.

Grady flew several different schedules; the most often used was very early morning until noon, the early afternoon until seven o'clock, or the afternoon until midnight or much later. Betty routinely slept late then went into town, usually ate at the drug store, then window shopped. She loved the stores of downtown Tampa. They had a "tremendous MAAS Brothers Store" which had all the latest fashions in ladies' clothing.

For supper, Betty would take the bus to the air force base and eat with Grady in the officers' mess. It cost thirty-nine cents. If Grady was flying late or was in class, he would bring them a BLT from the drug store across the street from their room. "We didn't seem to have a lot to eat but we could keep fruit in the room if it didn't attract ants." Her description of the situation is faithful to life as she lived it. "I indeed had a two-month honeymoon."

March 8, 20:00:

One month and no diary. Tsk, tsk, tsk! Rosey, get on the ball. This has really been a big month for me. Probably the biggest of my whole life. Betty finally talked me into getting married. Sad story. We were married—oh well, read it here [newspaper clipping].

Truthfully, I can say the past two weeks have been the most wonderful of my life. I don't see why I haven't tried this married life before. It's really the stuff. Eh, Mother? We stayed at the Floridan Hotel for the first five days, which knocked a hole in our income for the next five months. We're now living in a room out on Rome Avenue (twin beds, one never used) it isn't the best in the world but we're happy enough with this married life. I'm going to enjoy it instead of writing about it. I wish I could describe it but it is just impossible; you'll have to try it for yourself sometime.

The crew is really trucking along. We have around sixty hours of flying time. We went on a bombing run this morning. The bombardier is red hot. We dropped ten bombs on a wharf at Melagee. We finished with a GE of ninety-one. And two direct hits. Pretty good, eh?

We came back to the field to land at 1200 hours and found it closed to the ground by a line squall. The other ship that I was flying formation with went to Hendricks Field and landed. We landed around 1330 hours. We ate dinner there and messed around operations until 1630 hours. I saw Jeanne, Kit Hall, Margie Alexander, and some more of the personnel there. It seemed like good old times to be back at Hendricks. I certainly liked that field.

We departed from Hendricks and landed at Drew Field at 1730 hours. The ceiling was at one thousand feet when we landed. We were the only ship to make it back this afternoon.

March 11, Saturday, 21:30:

I got home a little earlier than usual tonight. It's raining straight down outside. I like the change though. Reminds me of some of the good old weather in Chattanooga.

Betty really looks sweet tonight. I'll never forget how dainty and refreshing she looked in the dimmed lights of our "adoring" little room. I had two letters from Mother today.

I had an interesting flight last night. We went to New Orleans, direct over the water. The clouds were low and we went through heavy rain most of the time. It was tough navigating but McClung, my navigator, got us there and back okay. We were supposed to have hit Ft. Myers coming back, but we hit Drew Field instead. Just as good though; besides, it was getting late. McClung certainly p-ed me off the last night we flew. We went in a high-altitude cross-country and on the return, instead of navigating, he flew the radio compass in. We ended up in Orlando, lost as a blind goose. We got back to the field a little late. He is a frazzling good navigator and seems to know his stuff, but he's relaxed a little too much. He's strictly okay though.

Well, I must talk to this sweet little girl here. Frank Sinatra is singing and she is swooning herself to death. Just what has he got that I haven't?

March 12, Sunday, 16:20:

Rain, rain, and more rain. Will it never stop? Betty and I went out to Drew Field to go to chapel this morning. As usual, we were too late. I was an hour late for my wedding. We ate lunch at the officers club. Very good meal. We rode back into town with a friend, Lt. Wood. We're going to church together tonight.

I have to get up in the morning at 0300 hours to fly. I won't get to spend the night here with Betty. Cob it all. I think this is a rough war. I think we are going down to the bay for a little while; want to come along? Let's go.

March 13, 21:00:

What a day, oh, what a day! We flew this morning. I was lead ship in a four-ship formation. We were to fly at high altitude. We got out to our ships and started up okay. Number two engine ran a little rough and was a little hard to get started. We called the tower for the instruction. They informed us the field was closed for low stratus clouds. After standing by for about an hour, we were given an instrument clearance.

We were supposed to have assembled over the TM code of silence above the overcast. We got off a little earlier than the other boys and churned up through the overcast. That was one of the most beautiful sights I have ever seen as we broke through the top of that overcast. It was just a rolling bumpy floor of white velvet as far as one could see. We skimmed across the top like a—well, like something.

After circling for about an hour, two of the ships finally joined me in formation. We circled for another forty-five minutes, waiting for Rudow in the other plane. We received several radio messages but he was unable to locate us. We decided to go on up without him. We climbed to about 8,900 ft. and Reid, on the right wing, left the formation with engine trouble. That left Phillips and me to fly formation. We leveled off at ten thousand feet to allow our engines to cool and to wait a little while longer for Rudow.

After flying around for about ten minutes, we started climbing again. My #2 engine started to sputter oil. I didn't know whether to feather it or just what to do. At sixteen thousand feet, I decided to go back to the field. We left Phillips and descended. As we were going down, oil began to pour out so I feathered and came in on three engines.

I think all the boys belong to the "Drew Field Feather Club." These rotten planes stink. I had to go see Capt. Dortch, the group engineering officer. He tried to pin it on me. I know I'll have to see Maj. Ferguson. I don't mind though. I did what I thought was right though. Cob Major and the whole outfit.

Betty's working on something over here. Looks interesting (remember Betty).

March 14, 22:00:
Everything happens to Rozzell. We flew this afternoon. I wasn't scheduled to fly but around 1700 hours, Lt. Philpot assigned us a ship. We had two hours so we went to Homosassa Springs to bomb.

We went out, started up, and took off. Everything was fine. We were climbing up when Morin called up that his tables were back on the ground.

Headache! Luck was with us. Morin remembered the trail and disc speed when we bombed at 8,500 at Nolagee. Clouds and mist nearly enveloped the target. We made several dry runs and finally got out six bombs.

We came on back to the field a half-hour late. I let Lucketti bring the ship in on the traffic pattern. He came in on the base leg about a mile from the field. When I landed, the tower called and told me to report to the tower officer. I was really befuddled; I didn't know whether it was for the sloppy entrance in the pattern, for low approach, for turning off the runway before the end of the strip.

I found out though. It was for the pattern entrance. The tower officer chewed me a little. All I said was yes, sir, and no, sir. I told him the entrance was terrible and he agreed with me. I told him it wouldn't happen again, etc.

The boys couldn't find my oxygen mask when they left the ship so I am without a mask that I need so badly. I don't know how I am going to get another one and I'm too sleepy to care much. Good night.

March 16, 09:30:

This is all so unbelievable. I slept until a few minutes ago. I say again, this is wonderful. I don't have to go to the field until 11:00. I just don't believe it. Yesterday was a pretty good day. We had intelligence in ground school yesterday morning. I had all afternoon off until 15:00. Then I was supposed to have had Link for two hours. I went to Link and they canceled that. Naturally, I came home early.

Betty and I went down to the bay and fed the seagulls. We had a good time. Those babies can really fly. Betty has just returned from the drug store with something to eat. Shall we?

March 21, Tuesday, 21:30:

Time is whizzing by. Betty is making my stay here in the states all too short. We're happy though.

I ran completely off the runway last Thursday night. Lucky left the tail wheel on unlocked. I should have seen the big red light on the dash panel but I had my head up and locked. Thirty-seven thousand pounds is a lot of airplane to go zig-zagging all over the field.

Boy, was I p-ed off Sunday. My day off and Maj. Ferguson makes us report to the flight line at 1130 hours. When we got there, Lt. Pebes gave us a lecture on the duties of an airplane commander. Lt. Pebes is my new flight commander. I've been changed to the E Flight. I hated to lose Lt. Philpot he was a swell boy.

To make it all the worse I've found out that we were supposed to fly Sunday night. When we went down to fly though, they told us we wouldn't have to because we were so far ahead on our bombs. I couldn't find the crew anyway. We flew last night and dropped twenty more bombs. Lt. Viar commended us on our good work.

I'm having a little trouble getting my crew arranged. Gasgue, my original engineer, was grounded. I'm getting Smeallie, asst. Engineer, transferred to engineer, and I'm getting Ivey, asst. armor, transferred to asst. engineer. While the transfer was going through, processing assigned me another engineer, Haskell. Now I'm trying to get Haskell removed and everything straightened out. Problems and more problems.

March 23, Thursday, 11:00:

Yes, sir, I've been married a month today, and do I love it.

Yeah, man! This has been the shortest month of my life. These last two days are almost unbelievable. I've slept until 10:00 both mornings. We were supposed to have flown last night, but flying was called off because of the weather. Too bad!

March 26, 23:00:

Am I burning up tonight! We went to St. Petersburg and went swimming at the Pass-a-Grille Beach on the Gulf of Mexico. Lucketti went with us. We certainly had a swell time, but believe me, we are paying for it now, and how. I don't think it is going to be too bad though.

This payday had better start rolling around and fast. A few more days and we'll have to go to the soup line.

I thought we'd never get on that bus tonight. It was loaded to the brim. Betty's about under the weather. I know exactly how she feels.

March 29, 20:00:

We're finishing up fast here now. We flew formation again today. I was the lead ship of a six-ship formation. It's a lot of fun to have more than three ships but it's a little harder to keep together. I'll be glad when we get to England and have hundreds of ships, no big problem.

Smealie made some pictures today. I'll show them to you in a few days, okay?

March 30, 21:00:

My crew went ditching today. We didn't get to get in the water though, it was too cold. We got a chance to go to the Gulf Sunday and ride on the rafts under actual conditions.

April 4, 16:00:

April Fool's Day and How! What a day April 1 was. The entire 396th Bomb Crew Section was restricted to the post until April 6. Yeah! I know today is just the fourth but I had to come home to see my wife. I just hope I don't get caught when I go back tonight. I think it's worth it though. I'll take the chance gladly.

Sunday was an interesting day. We went to the Gulf of Mexico to take pictures for the Ditching Dept. Five of my crew went. Lucketti, McClung, Smeallie, and Riep. We rode a big GI truck to Clearwater. At Clearwater, we boarded a big one-hundred-foot Coast Guard cutter for the open sea. The skipper let me pilot her most of the way out. It was a lot of fun but not as hard to handle as the old B-17, no sirree.

We went out, I don't know how far, and cut the throttles. The boat rocked like a mad man. It was really rolling. We inflated and put rafts overboard. After a few minutes of preparation, we boarded the two rafts and cut loose from the ship. We paddled around letting the photographer make pictures. He made pictures of us tying together, putting up the sail, dealing out rations, etc.

I really got a big kick out of the cameraman. He would make pictures a while then go vomit for a few minutes. He got so sick he finally quit making pictures and spent all his time vomiting. Everyone in our raft made out okay, except Lucky—he got a little sick and heaved over the side. Personally, I think the trip was a good experience as well as a lot of fun.

Friday was payday. A very sweet day too. Betty and I had $.60 together.

April 6, 20:00:

Home again! Whew, I certainly hope I don't get caught coming home during this restriction. I've got to see Betty though. We went to Savannah, Georgia, yesterday in a camera attack mission. We went in a six-ship formation at altitude. I must say we nearly froze. It was twenty degrees below 0°C. My feet nearly froze. We got four camera attacks. We're almost through now. I'll be glad too. Maybe I can spend a little time with Betty. It's cold here in Florida.

April 7, 21:00:

Good Friday, oh! Boy, I checked out a new B-17G plane today. It is a honey. I rode with Capt. Concannon. The new G flies more like an airplane than the F. We may get a new one for keeps in a few days. I hope so. We got three more camera attacks this morning. All we need to finish is a gunnery mission, which I hope we get tomorrow. This getting up every morning at 0230 hours and flying at altitude is about to get me down.

April 8, Saturday, 21:30:

It is finished. It is finished. Yes sirree, my little crew finished flying today. We had a mission this morning. We flew with Rudow. We met a B-26 towing target ship and climbed to twenty thousand feet to shoot. I haven't been so p-ed off for a long time. We nearly killed each other flying formation. The top turret and ball turret would not operate after we go up there. I thought we'd never get the rounds fired but we did. McClung tried to drop bombs. I'll take my bombardier next time, eh, Mc?

April 9, Easter Sunday, 22:00:

What a day. Betty is all tired out. We went to chapel this morning. We ate dinner at the officers club. Lt. Morin, my bombardier, had dinner with us. We went to church tonight at the First Baptist Church.

They did an Easter Cantata. Lt. Morin's wife went home Saturday. I think he'll be a sad sack. She's going to have a baby.

Oh! I have a new crew member: S/Sgt. Brally. He is certainly a good man. He's had over five hundred flight hours.

April 11, Tuesday, 22:00:

Well, do say! I just don't believe it—nope, I just can't believe it. Well, believe it or not, but I'm going home on leave. Get those bags packed, honey, and let's board the Chattanooga choo-choo. I'll finish clearing the field in the morning and we'll leave tomorrow afternoon. This is all too wonderful, but I suspect it's the truth. It's going to be grand being home. The only thing I dread about going home is leaving to come back. Believe me. Well, excuse me for about a week, I'm not going to take time to write in this thing. No sirree.

April 21, Friday, 23:00:

Well, here we are again, Cob it. All these leaves pass just all too fast. Those eight days seem like just a dream. I mean, I thoroughly enjoyed them. It was wonderful to see all the folks and friends again.

Betty and I stayed with my parents up in Middle Tennessee. They live out on the job where Dad works. I went around on the job with Dad several times. He is the best dad in the world and I know Mother is the best mom that anyone could possibly have.

We went to LaFayette to see Betty's parents Monday and spent the night there. We brought Turbo, my monkey, back from Chattanooga to Oak Ridge with us. He and Dad are great friends. We went to the mountains Wednesday morning and stayed until Thursday morning. I saw all my aunts and cousins, etc. I was very fortunate to see Levere. He was in on leave from California. He's a member of the Anti-Aircraft Unit. A very nice-looking fellow too.

Needless to say, we're pretty tired tonight. We were lucky to get a seat up and back on the train but we managed.

This Betty of mine is the sweetest person. I love her more and more every day.

April 22, Saturday, 22:00 (last night with Betty):
I must say I wish they wouldn't rush things so much. We're leaving
Drew Field tomorrow afternoon. I don't give a hoot for leaving Drew
Field, I certainly hate to leave Betty. Betty has become a big part of me,
I love her more than I could ever imagine loving anyone.

They really screwed me up today. Riep hasn't returned so they told
me I wouldn't leave today. About five o'clock they decided I would have
to clear. Most of the places closed, so I will have to clear tomorrow.

I am going to spend these last few precious moments with Betty.

Betty said of the leave, "We went home on leave for two
weeks. We rode the train to Chattanooga. Frank [Grady's father]
met us. Frank took us to Oak Ridge where he was superintendent of residential construction. The houses the workers lived in
were double-wide trailers with two bedrooms, one restroom,
and a small kitchen, living room, dining room combination. The
neighborhood had shower houses like campgrounds.

"Grandmother Savage [Grady's mother, Louisa's, mother]
lived with them. Louisa worked in the meat market part of the
company grocery store. Peggy [Grady's sister] was at school and
when Grady went out with Frank, I was left there to cook. I
couldn't boil water. Grandmother Savage taught me enough to
get through the stay. Louisa's last word before leaving for work
that first morning was 'Don't fix deviled eggs.' When it came to

fix supper, Grandmother Savage looked at me and said, 'Let's fix deviled eggs.'"

Betty wanted to visit her mother and dad so, toward the end of the first week, Betty and Grady rode the bus into Chattanooga and then on to LaFayette. The visit ended and they took the same bus and route back toward Oak Ridge. Betty here told a story that she repeated often: "We were getting close to Oak Ridge and Grady got anxious and kept insisting it was time to 'pull the cord' for us to get off. I knew it wasn't and kept telling him that I knew when to pull the cord. Finally, after much of his insisting it was time, I 'pulled the cord' and we bailed out with a full B4 bag. I was in three-inch heels. We walked two miles to Frank's house in mud.

The monkey situation was a sore subject and I never at any time was able to start a conversation with Grady about it. Betty and Grady's sister, Peggy Campbell, talked some about it but most of what I know is glued-together pieces.

Sometime in early April, Grady decided the crew needed a mascot to fly with them on missions, something like a "good-luck charm." Grady found a pet dealer in Tampa who had the monkey and Grady fell in love with him. He purchased the monkey and socialized him with the crew for a few days. As happens in a military family, the ruling class heard of the monkey, named Turbo by now, and gently explained to Grady that it was against all regulation concerning military operation, and Air Force regulation, in particular, to take pets of any kind on missions.

The easiest solution of the monkey-ownership problem would be to leave Turbo with Grady's father in Tennessee while Grady was overseas. So when Grady and Betty went home on leave, they took Turbo with them. It seemed to Grady that his dad, Frank, really liked the monkey and so his problems were solved. Betty and Grady went back to Florida, without Turbo, to finish preparations for Grady's departure for the European Theater of War.

I never heard a word from Frank about the monkey. He may have been happy with the little thing, but not very long after Grady left for England, Turbo bit Grady's sister, Peggy. Frank could tolerate a lot of things but abuse of his favorite daughter was not one of them. Betty was back in Georgia with her parents so Frank took the monkey to her and asked her to take care of the offending little animal.

Betty's father, Carlos, knew what to do with Turbo. Carlos went to his shop and built a wooden framed shipping crate covered with one-inch-square chicken wire. He took the animal in the crate to the post office in Trion, Georgia. Carlos then fastened the name and address of the pet store in Tampa, Florida, where Grady had purchased the animal and sent him back to Florida.

There is conflicting evidence concerning the recovery of Turbo's purchase price, but I am confident that at least part of the cost was recovered.

April 23, Sunday, 21:00:

On board the train to Hunter Field, Savannah. Here's goodbye to Florida, maybe. We boarded this train around 1900 hours this evening and, to my great surprise, we have a nice car to ride in. It's a special troop sleeper. There's deck beds with the first and second decks forming a seat and back of seat; it's rather cozy.

Oh, I hated to leave Betty today. I don't know how I can make out without her. She's a darling. She came out to the field and had dinner with me at the officers club. I kissed her goodbye at the bus station at 16:29:30 sec. Goodbye to the dearest and most precious girl in the world.

Betty said of the departure, "Grady was packing to leave as soon as we got back to Tampa. I went with him to the train station and after a final kiss watched him ride away."

She then went into downtown Tampa and "bought a flower

for my hair." She then walked back to her room at 828 Rome Avenue, "got my suitcase packed, and went back into town to the bus station."

Betty caught "the first bus going to Georgia and went home." She got into Trion around two a.m. and was able to get a cab to Center Post. The cab cost "two dollars, I think, and I don't know where I would have gotten two dollars."

She worked the "time Grady was overseas. They gave me a key to the office and I typed reports until the other employees got in the office."

Was she concerned for Grady's safety? "Although the statistics showed that seven of ten planes were lost, I never doubted he would come home. There were many couples getting married before the men shipped out. One common statement of the girls was, 'I never knew whether I was a bride or a widow.'"

April 24, Monday, 21:00: Hunter Field, Savannah, Georgia

Arrived here this morning around 07:00. Had a pleasant trip, or I reckon I did, I slept all the way. We stopped by the billeting office, drew bedding and room assignments. We went to get processed this afternoon but just barely did get started. This field really has good organization. They seem to know just what the score is. That's more than I can say about Drew Field. That was the most disorganized place I've ever seen.

There's a big, lonely spot in my heart tonight. My, how I miss Betty.

April 25, Tuesday, 23:30:

Bang! Bang! Thank you, man! That's about the way you go through this place. I have no bitches to make about this field. They are really on the ball. We went through processing this morning and shown down inspection this afternoon. They checked and issued more stuff today. I have a new .45 Colt pistol. And a new hack watch, parachute, and a new A-14 oxygen mask, which is really a honey. Well, I even have a new airplane, a new B-17G. She's a peach. I'll have to get me a name for her.

It seems as if I'd left Betty months ago. Darling, you'll never know how much I miss you. You're wonderful.

April 26, Wednesday, 22:00:

We went down to test hop our new plane this morning but the weather held us down to the ground. I'll certainly be glad to finish here and get on to where I'm going. I'm getting eager to come back home, yes, sir. I have a beautiful girl waiting for me. I must say I have every-thing to come back to—meaning you, Betty.

It has rained all day long. My, I wish it would clear up. It's so dull and lonesome tonight, I can hardly stand it. My heart aches for Betty.

April 27, Thursday, 22:45:

Oh, boy, is it a honey. We tried our new ship out today. I don't know what I'm saying. I must be thinking of Betty as usual.

We went on the a/speed calibration range today. Did we have fun. That was about all the buzzing I've done since I've been in the army. We flew up and down the railroad track between two towns. I'd sure hate to have been in one of those towns with airplanes buzzing over my head all day. No, maybe I'd love that. I know I love Betty. Yep, I'm sure of that. I wish I could see you tonight, darling.

April 28, Friday, 22:00: Ft. Dix, New Jersey

My, my, but how you get around, Rosey. We left Hunter Field about 13:30 this afternoon and arrived here at Ft. Dix about 18:30. We had a nice trip. Coming up, we passed over several states: Georgia, South Carolina, North Carolina, Virginia, Delaware, Dist. of Columbia, Pennsylvania, and are now in New Jersey.

It's a little chilly here, I must say. I like it though, it's just pleasant.

The Capitol Dome at Washington was really an inspiring sight. It'll be more inspiring, though, when I see it on the way back home. I've put several miles between Betty and me but she's still with me.

April 29, Saturday, 22:30: Greiner Field, New Hampshire

We left Ft. Dix around 10:30 this morning and arrived here at Greiner Field around 1400 hours. I'm really up in Yankee territory now. I think I'll put in for foreign duty pay.

The trip up here was something else. I haven't seen so much in such a short time before in my life. Easton, Lucky's hometown—I mean, we really laid a buzz job on his home. I'll bet his people thought the world was coming to an end when all four roared down at their house. After leaving Easton, we went back east a ways to get on the airways. In an hour or so, we approached New York City. My, what a place. I didn't know they could pile concrete so high. New York is even bigger than Chattanooga. I thought the Empire State Building was going to take off a wing and we were flying at three thousand feet. I'll never forget that massive place. I'm coming back to see it from the ground sometime.

Up from Manhattan stood one of the most inspiring sights I've ever seen. I'd heard a lot about it, I knew it was there but really I'd never thought much about seeing it and especially I had never thought about seeing it from the air as a pilot of a Flying Fortress on its way to win a war, but things happen in unexpected ways. Just like the last time, I got married. I would have thought someone was crazy if they even thought I'd get married, but I did and am I glad of it, I must say I am. Yes, sir! There in the harbor stood the Statue of Liberty, silent yet so meaningful. It really gave one a feeling to pay for the stuff one has to go through with to win a war. Another sight I'll never forget.

After leaving New York, we went farther north through Connecticut, over Massachusetts, and here is New Hampshire. The landscape up through here is beautiful. Reminds me of the dear old state of Tennessee with hills galore. This field is down in a valley. I came right over the top of a hill and then had to drop down to land on the field. We made it, though.

A station wagon met us shortly after we landed and brought us into a processing building. We went through a few lines as usual and then came to our BOQ. We attended briefing tonight on the North Atlantic route so I'm almost certain of going to England.

April 30, Sunday, 22:30:

Another day of rest. These army Sundays aren't spent like the ones I used to spend as a civilian. I used to go to church on Sunday morning and Sunday evening too. In the army, I'm lucky if I get to go to chapel on Sunday morning. This morning, I had Link Trainer for half an hour right at chapel period. I flew a procedure let down on the Prestwick range that we'll use when we land in England. I expected to leave this morning, but I suspect not. Oh, well! We'll have some time. I got a little pay today—nice, eh? I sent it to my wife.

May 1, Monday, 22:15:

Still here at Greiner Field. I just knew we'd leave today but I was fooled. Most of the other fellows did leave. I'm stuck here, a bad flux gate compass and shot altimeter. The compass was fixed today but the altimeter was still out tonight. I hope they fix it tonight so we can leave tomorrow.

We went to the skeet range this afternoon and then to the pistol range. I tried out my pistol, "Bittie the Lady." She really works swell.

I like her and I know I like Betty. I mean, I like her. She's the sweetest girl in all the world. I hope to leave in the morning. Let's both hope.

May 2, Tuesday:

Left Grenier Field, arrived Gander Field, Newfoundland, en route to Gander by B-17G 42-297673, 0500 hours. Boys, this is it! The colored orderly just awakened me, transportation will be up after us at 06:00 to take us to the final briefing and then we'll be gone. Yep, we're off to war.

09:00: We're ready to taxi out to takeoff position. I've just called the tower. We're to use runway 18 (due south t.o.)

09:30: *We're airborne now, traveling at an altitude of three thousand feet. We're supposed to fly at seven thousand but I'm staying down so we can buzz Morin's home at Lewiston, Massachusetts. I last felt good US soil at 09:05:30 sec. We're having a little trouble with the Leason Set. En route to Newfoundland.*

10:05: *We've just finished making three runs at Morin's home. On the third run, I spied a radio tower, and did I pull up and get away. From that place. I hope they didn't get our number. We are flying with the IFF on. I hope she works when we leave the US.*

10:25: *We are now at seven thousand feet on course for Bangor, Massachusetts. We have the AFCE (automatic pilot) set up. It works marvelously. It's certainly a lifesaver.*

10:40: *We're well up in the state of Maine now. We've been trying to contact Bangor Control with little success. Our code is Copra Mike. Down below are beautiful lakes and very "woody" woodlands. The lakes are beginning to be covered with ice. In the far left, I get my first glimpse of a snow-capped mountain, Tassadem Kay.*

10:50: *Whew! At the ice on the lakes below. The mountain is a majestic-looking thing over there in her white covering of snow.*

11:20: *Radio room—Lucky, Morin, Burnett, Smitty, and I are back in the radio room having dinner. Smeallie and Ivey are in the pilot's compartment watching the airplane. Good crew I have. About six of them can fly the airplane straight and level. For the first time in a long time, I'm drinking a cup of coffee. Maybe I should say I'm having a little coffee with my sugar.*

11:45: *I'm taking my last long look at the best country in the world. I wonder how long it will be before I see her again. Soon, I hope. Boy, this is hard. Oh, well! Someone must fight this war. All I can say is that there's a mighty good crew coming over.*

11:51: *We're now leaving the last of Canada. There's a lot of water down there.*

12:10: *Off to the left are the Prince Edward Islands.*

12:45: *From the pilot's seat, I can look down at the Magdalen Islands. It has long inlets and channels. The walls dropped off like ice and crack off and left large cliffs. Part of the terrain still has its winter* *blanket of snow. The black crevices are ugly things. How and why any-one lives here is beyond me.*

13:00: *We're out over the Gulf of St. Lawrence in 150 miles of ice water, and I mean ice water. The crew all have out their Mae West. In the far right distance, I can see the Anguille Mountains high and beau-tiful with its snow-clad sides protruding abruptly through the other-wise unobstructed horizon.*

13:30: *The mountains are off just to the right now. Snow-topped plateaus, crevices, reddish sheer banks, all tops are flat. Part of the win-ter's snow has melted leaving black-topped ridges streaking the snow-white. It looks cold, bleak, and very uninviting.*

13:45: *Just received a weather report from Gander that visibility seven-eighths-mile, two-thousand-foot ceiling. Looks like we'll have to make an instrument approach between the mountains.*

13:54: *We have just passed over the airport of Stephenville (code name Jasper) and have taken up a heading of seventy-six degrees for Gander. Gander is on the other side of Newfoundland. My, how I'd hate to go down in these ridges. Mustn't think of such things. Strictly against good training. A small frozen river is twisting and winding under us. It looks like a large white snake. A large C-54 is scooting un-der us. I wish we were heading in that direction. Another aircraft is reported twelve miles away at 12:00.*

14:05: *We are over the forks of two large rivers. Low cumulus clouds are floating underneath. It looks like a low ceiling ahead.*

14:22: *At Buchans Plateau taken a heading of eighty degrees to make Gander. This is a really beautiful, country. That is, from up here it looks beautiful.*

14:30: *There's the field out there. No low ceiling or nothing of the kind. Thank goodness.*

14:40: *We've arrived over the field and circled it twice to the left. I've received land instruction and altimeter setting from the tower. We're to land on runway 36 (due north landing). The altimeter setting is Yoke Uncle. Sound like Greek to you? Or if you had the secret code that we do, it figures out to be 30.28.*

15:15: *We landed at 15:08. A good landing too, I must say. We've* *just finished cutting off the engines. Rather cold here. I can take it, I hope.*

22:00: In BOQ. Mother wouldn't believe it, but I have on my long handles. It isn't so cold here just a little chilly. I read my secret order. Eighth Air Force, London, England. We go to a briefing tomorrow 1300 hours

May 3, Wednesday, 23:30: Gander Field, Newfoundland

Well, everything happens to us. Lucketti's in the hospital with a cold or something. I don't know when we'll get to leave here. We're getting seven dollars per day—per diem. I'd rather get on over to England and get it over with. I'm anxious to get back home. I saw the B-29s here on this field. They're beautiful things. It looks just like an overgrown B-17. Besides, they've torn all the runways up around here. We went to briefing at 1300 hours and were briefed on our flight from here to Scotland. It is flown at night, about a twelve-hour flight—long time, no sleep!

May 4, Thursday, 23:10: Gander Field, Newfoundland

Oh, my poor aching legs. I've walked a hundred miles today. Since Lucketti's in the hospital we've decided to make the best of it so we called special services this morning for something to do. We ended up going fishing. After getting all the instructions for finding the lake, and after walking for about two hours, we found the lake. It was frozen over with snow covering the ice. We had a swell time playing and falling through the snow, but no fish.

Oh, what I wouldn't give to see Betty.

May 5, Friday: Gander Field, Newfoundland

It's misting outside. I wish to goodness it would snow. I haven't seen snow this winter. It doesn't snow much in Florida.

I have just returned from the hospital. Lucketti will be out just anytime now. They have all the runways torn up now. I don't know whether we can leave or not. I can't get used to these crazy people up here driving on the left-hand side of the road. I think they're going to run over me every time I get on the road.

I haven't had any mail for two weeks. I'm telling you, I'd like to hear from some people I know.

May 6, Saturday, 24:00: Gander Field Newfoundland

Am I going nuts. If I'm not, I soon will be. I think the fellows stationed at this field gradually go crazy. We were going to eat tonight and passing by a barrack, we heard a funny noise. It turned out to be one of the boys playing choo-choo. On the way back to the barracks, a boy ran past us weaving from one side of the road to the other. They call it being "Ganderized."

Betty would love this—the boy going like a train was from Georgia, her dear home state. Speaking of Georgia, I'd certainly like to be there now and how, wouldn't I, Betty.

May 7, Sunday, 00:00:

Another day of rest. I've enjoyed this day a little better than the rest. Riep, Smeallie, Ivey, and I went to chapel this morning. We had a good sermon by a Canadian chaplain. After going to chapel, most of the crew went to the Canadian gymnasium. Brailley and I passed a baseball for half an hour. Morin and I went to the officers club for a little while this afternoon. That's really a dead place.

Lucky will be out of the hospital tomorrow. Maybe we'll get to leave tomorrow night. Betty, I certainly missed you today. In fact, I miss you every day, every hour.

May 8: Gander Field, Newfoundland

09:00: Well, look who's here. Yep, it's Lucky, out of the hospital. Rosey, let's get down to operations and see if we can't leave this place. Okay by me.

09:31: *It looks as if our stay here will be very short now. We've just returned from briefing and we're all set to go. I have all the weather codes, flight clearances, etc. All we have to do is load in the plane and take off. We're supposed to land in Prestwick, Scotland.*

19:50: *Here we go on our last hop in this new baby. She's a good plane. I hope she gets us to Scotland. We took off at 1944 hours. We had to run up our watches two hours before we left.*

20:00: *We're leaving the last of Newfoundland. There's over two thousand miles between here and Scotland. Let's get on the ball. There's a few icebergs in the water below. The sun's reflection makes them bright as light. Very beautiful.*

21:50: *We've leveled off at nine thousand feet, some two hundred miles of water has been spanned. The good old autopilot is working wonderfully. Boy, I really love that thing. The best friend I have. Thin stratus clouds are drifting underneath. I'm reading a little handbook on customs in England.*

22:14: *The sun is gliding down below, the far distant horizon leaving a vivid gold border across the tip of a low-lying stratus-form cloud. It's impossible to see the cold, cold water below. Tall, finger-like columnar clouds are reaching up for us. I hope it doesn't develop into something. We're prepared for the worst though.*

22:52: *I see the moon and the moon sees me. Yep, there she is out there in the far distance. A round yellow ball and a very heartwarming sight. It's getting dark. I'll have to turn on a few lights.*

May 9, Tuesday: en route to Prestwick, Scotland

02:00: *We've been flying through icy drizzle for the past hour. A little ice is accumulating on the wing, nothing serious.*

02:50: *This is really beautiful. We have broken out over the top of a lower undercast. The full moon up to the right makes it look like a big platter of divinity candy.*

Speaking of divinity! We're transferring fuel. When we left Gander, we had 2,700 gallons of gas or enough to last for fourteen hours.

03:15: *I have just turned on the Beloek Range. The son of a ---ing*

Germans are playing grand opera right on the range. Wouldn't that piss you off? I can't hear worth.

04:30: Am I enjoying this. We're riding about ten feet above the level floor of a blanket of stratus clouds. Just like buzzing.

04:50: In the far distant left, the sun is peeping through, making one golden globe. Occasionally, I can get a glance at the dark water through the thick walls of clouds. I'll just stay up here, thank you

05:30: Just look down through that, would you. Land. Yes, I think the most beautiful land I've ever seen, green rolling fields.

06:00: I'm going to have to make an instrument approach using the radio. The clouds are too thick and low. Let's get busy, Rosey.

22:00: We landed here at Prestwick, Scotland, this morning at 0700 hours. I'm here at Adamton House all alone. The rest of the crew went on to Stone. I have to stay here until they check the airplane for shortages. It took us 11:20 to fly over here.

The Adamton House was built in 1883 as a private estate. The grounds and history of the estate date to the eleventh century.

At the start of the war, the Adamton House was taken over by the British Military, then in April of 1943, the USAAF Air Transport Command took it as an administrative center and officers mess, serving its personnel based in or passing through Prestwick.

May 10, Wednesday, 14:00: Prestwick, Scotland

I slept this morning until 11:20. A Scottish woman woke me up singing, "Yank my doodle, it's a dandy. Yank my doodle till I die." I can hardly understand these Scots. I had my money changed to English money. Yesterday, I had pennies, nickels, and dimes, now I have pence, shillings, and pounds. I just give them a big coin and they give me back some little coins. I don't know whether I'm getting cheated or not.

This big house I'm staying in reminds me of books I've read. A grand, old English mansion. The stables cost more than my dad's house. They have a PX in the stable.

We're leaving tonight at 17:30 to join our crews at Stone. There's three other first pilots here besides myself. I really miss my crew just this one night. I know someone else that I really miss. I really wish she was over here to enjoy this with me. Did I say enjoy? Oh, well! It is fun in a way. Everything is new and strange.

May 11, Thursday, 23:00: 8th AFRD Stone, England

Arrived here by train this morning around 09:00. What a train ride. These English cars are about half the size of the American cars and about half the size of the American coaches—each coach is divided into several compartments and no aisles. We changed trains four times before we finally got here.

The British have been at war for over four years and the man shortage is acute. Hence no railroad porters. So each train change we had to lug our bags for about a half-mile. Yes, it was very funny. We had all our clothes, plus full flying equipment. Well, I'm glad we made it. We're going to be staying here for four or five days and then we'll go to our permanent station. I'll be glad to get settled in a permanent place.

We stopped in Glasgow, Scotland, for about two hours. These cities don't impress me. The children all ask, "Chum gum?" They wanted chewing gum.

May 12, Friday, 24:00:
This has been rather a full day. We had a few orientation lectures this morning from the CO, the chaplain, and of course, a venereal disease lecture from the medics. This afternoon we went to Beaty Hall for gas lectures. We were issued our new lightweight gas mask. They are quite an improvement over the old type.

After getting fitted with masks, we had a short physical. As usual, I needed a shot. It was tetanus this time. Boy, I thought my arm was coming off. Lucky and I went to Hanley tonight. It's a city about eighteen miles from here. The girls are terrible there. Two got on our trail as soon as we landed there. I'm not going back. I don't want to get raped. We went to Henley PX for a while. Lucky found him a redheaded girl and I had to be content with leading her dog. Useless pilot!

May 13, Saturday, 22:00: Stone, England
Most of the boys went to town again tonight. I stayed in. I'm almost afraid to go to town. Those English girls.

I had an interesting job this morning. The old mail censor. I've never been in so many moods in one morning in my life. I bitched with the bitcher, loved with the lover, got home sick with the lonely and I'm a hearty sympathizer with the widowers. I hope I never get this job again. At least not very often.

May 14, Sunday, 20:00: Stone, England, Mother's Day
I attended chapel this morning at Howard Hall. We heard a sermon on love. I wish I could be with my mother this Mother's Day, and how!

We had a real show by the P-38s today. They nearly tore the place apart. We're on shipping orders to leave in the morning at 08:45.

May 15, Monday: Deenethorpe AAF Station 128

Arrived here this afternoon at 1500 hours. This is to be our place of business for a few months. There were seven crews sent here as replacements for the 401st bomb group. My crew was the only replacement for the 614th bomb squadron.

I met the squadron commander, Maj. Hinkle. He took me over to see the operations officer Maj. Garland. Both seem to be swell fellows. I've met a few of the fellows here. They treat us nice. All the talk tonight is about missions for our benefit and as answer to our thousands of questions. I mean, we ask plenty. Two P-38 instructors from the states moved in our room before we left Beaty Hall last night. We talked until around 01:00; they were transferred to P-47s and were they bitter.

One of the fellows I met this afternoon was Lt. Taylor. He returned from a mission to Berlin on the shelf the other day. In other words, he was shot down and flew home ten to fifty feet above the ground.

Deenethorpe is a village in Northamptonshire, England. For the war effort of WWII, it was designated RAF Deenethorpe and airfield for American heavy bombers. It was home to the 401st bomb group, a member of the 8th Air Force, from November 3, 1943, until June 20, 1945. For US military purposes, each airport was called a group. The USAAF designated the facility Station 128. The bombers were B-17Gs. The tail code for the 401st bomb group was a yellow triangle S. The facility was nine miles northeast of the town of Kettering. The 401st was the group farthest north in England, which was often described as an island aircraft carrier because there were so many air force facilities there during the war.

The 401st group was made up of four squadrons. They were the 612th (SC), the 613th (IN), the 614th (IW), and the 615th (IY). Each squadron was allocated eighteen aircraft (B-17G) but that number would vary depending on the mechanical condition of the planes and the availability of crews to fly them. When the entire squadron was deployed on a mission, they flew in six-plane formations with six planes in the lead "box," six planes in lower position "box," and six planes in a low "box." Pilots had to be flexible and fly where the squadron leader placed them and deploy with the squadron that needed them. The planes were subject to break down or damage from enemy fire, so the individual crew was also expected to fly any available plane. The crews were not always thrilled at the prospects of traveling in strange or unproven planes.

It required a huge outlay of manpower and materiel to keep the big bomber flying, crew members healthy, and ordnance supplied to planes in a timely manner.

In addition to the squadrons of crew members, the 401st also housed 18th Weather Detachment, which was housed on the bottom floor of the control tower. The weather in England was difficult to predict with the exception of the early morning heavy cloud cover. The early cloud cover was always there. When the cover was extremely bad and signs looked like it would last all morning or all day, it kept all planes on the ground.

The 450th Subdepot was the airplane repair department. A pilot and crew was only as good and effective as the quality of the airplane they flew. The mechanical crews made sure that the plane their crews flew was battle-worthy. The crews worked outside in whatever weather they were given; they worked whatever hours it required to get their aircraft ready for its next mission. The sheet metal crews patched holes the plane had come home with. They fixed and maintained the vital oil, fuel, electrical, and oxygen lines that ran through their machine. They worked over the big engines which kept the plane moving forward and on many occasions replaced the engines with a more dependable one. Each engine and plane was given a complete preflight check which meant working in early morning dampness and rain so that when the crew arrived, they had one less worry.

The bombs were handled by the 1579th Ordnance. There were always explosives on the base. At Deenethorpe, it was stored outside in a wooded area on the north side of base. The ordnance crew was also responsible for the machine guns and the ammunition used on the aircraft. Before every mission, the guns were attached and ammo inspected before the crew arrived.

Deenethorpe was not immune to medical needs. The flight crew required a special medical officer, the flight surgeon, and there was a hospital on site. To insure social order, the army detached the 1199th military police to the Deenethorpe village. The people who maintained and packed the parachutes had their office and workshop, and the 1209th Quartermaster Group took care of other supplies

Grady was assigned to the 614th Squadron. The call sign of the squadron was "golf club." The nickname was the "Lucky Devil." He told me that he did not recall any mission he flew that the 401st put more than fourteen crews in the air.

The 401st was a member of the 94th Combat Wing. A wing was a collection of three groups. In the case of the 94th, the groups, in addition to the 401st, were the 457th group at Glatton and the 351st group at Polebrook. The combat wing at full strength consisted of fifty-four aircraft.

The planes, when on a combat mission, flew in three boxes. The lead group in the middle and front of the formation was flown by the ranking member of the wing. One group flew above the lead group and to its left and the other group flew below the lead group and to its right. The dimensions of the wing "box" at perfect spacing were 2,300 yards wide by 600 yards deep by 2,900 yards top to bottom. These distances varied constantly due to combat circumstances. When there were several wings participating in a mission—and there usually were—there could be a six-mile interval between wings.

Norden bombsight on display at museum area of American Cemetery in Cambridge, England.

Grady did once explain to me in more detail how the bomb mission typically ran: "The lead squadron of each formation was always made up of the ranking officers. The highest-ranking, or commander, would be in the most forward plane of the V of that formation and the number one and number two plane of that unit were to the right of the commander. The number one and number two planes would carry the bombsights. That was the Norden bombsight. At the start of the war, the Norden bombsight was a highly secret device. They would carry them to the planes under armed guard. By the time I left, I think the Germans had as many of our Norden bombsights as we did.

"The reason for having the Norden on both the number one and number two planes was that in the event the number one plane got shot down, we had a backup. It was not as bad with the B-17G, like I flew, because it had the nose gun. Before that, the fighters would attack the most exposed lead planes nose on, and they took out quite a few.

"The lead plane was responsible for selecting the time and place to drop the bombs. There was a place on the route that was called the IP, I think it stood for intersection point. When we reached that point, the bombardier of the lead plane would connect to the automatic pilot of the plane and actually fly the plane to the target.

"The IP was forty to fifty miles from the target. The reason for that distance was to allow the formation to tighten up. We would often fly in such a close formation, I could see and effectively talk with the copilot and waste gunner in planes on our wings.

"At ten miles from the target, the lead plane would open his bomb doors. The other planes, of course, would open theirs when they saw the leader's doors open. This was also the last chance to adjust the plane's position. The pilot of the lead plane would switch the AFCE—which stood for 'Automatic Flight Control Equipment' but we called it the automatic pilot. This was linked with the Nordens which, in turn, would automatically drop the bombs from their bomb bays at the correct time. The other planes would not have the Norden and they would have to manually activate the bomb-release toggle switch. The second the other planes saw the bombs falling from the lead, they would trip their toggle switch and salvo the bomb load from all eighteen planes would fall on the target as one big mass for maximum destruction. Some of the crews still had bombardiers who would trip the toggle switch or be responsible for the Norden. I didn't have one since my bombardier had to take over as navigator with another crew.

"Now, of course, all the groups did not go to the same target. They would spread out the objectives to individual units depending on the size and strengths of the targets, except when we went to Berlin. There, we all dropped together on whatever the leader chose."

The 614th Squad logo; nickname was the Lucky Devil.

May 16, 22:00:

We got under way today. This morning the crew went through the hospital. After that, we went to base photo. There, we had our photo taken in civilian clothes to be used on identification cards if we're shot down over enemy territory. This afternoon we had all of our flying equipment checked. Now, all we have to do is go to ground school for a week and fly a few practice missions, then we'll be ready to go.

One of the fellows was really going to town last night. He had finished his combat missions and had been transferred to ATC. He and his army friends drank two bottles of whiskey that cost him fifteen dollars a bottle. He went after the third bottle this morning. The boys were scheduled for a mission this morning but it was scratched.

May 17, 23:00:

Rain, cold rain, won't it ever stop. I've never seen such weather as they have over here. One minute the sun shines so brightly and then the first thing you know, it is sleeting.

MISSION ONE

TUESDAY, MAY 30, 1944

The time had arrived and the preparation was to be tested. The 401st sent eighteen planes to lead the 94th CBW on this mission under the command of Lt. Col. Rogner. It was mission number seventy-nine for the 401st and mission number one for Grady. The crews of the 614th Squad were those of pilots Capt. A. H. Chapman, 1st Lt. W. R. Smith, 2nd Lt. A. L. Kilmer, 2nd Lt. W. G. Rozzell, 1st Lt. J. A. Gruman, 1st Lt. C. L. Wilson, and 2nd Lt G. L. La Fevor. The group's MPI was the assembly plant for the FW-190 aircraft in Oschersleben, Germany.

The strike photos showed that the bombing results were excellent. Range error and deflection were nonexistent. The bomb pattern covered the MPI with 50 percent of the strikes being within five hundred feet of center and 100 percent within two thousand feet of center.

Fairly accurate flack was encountered at the Drummer Lake region. The formation encountered between forty and sixty fighters as they left the target area, and two planes from the 614th were shot down. The crews who were lost and listed as MIA were those of pilots 1st Lt. C. L. Wilson and 2nd Lt. A. L. Kilmer. These two planes were flying in formation, one to the left wing and one to the right wing of Lt. Rozzell.

Grady's diary entry read:

May 30, Friday, 06:30:

Well, it looks as though this is it! We're assembled here at the plane, all set to start engines for our first combat mission. Our target for today is a FW-190 fighter plant at Oschersleben, Germany. We're loaded with ten 500-pound demolition bombs. The name of our airplane is "Shade Ruff." There's one thing that I like about it. It has Betty written all over the chin turret.

Lt. Shultz is riding as copilot today. He has been on missions before. They always send an experienced copilot with a crew on its first mission. Briefing for a mission is something. There is really a lot of suspense waiting on the curtain to go up to see where the mission's going. We found out. Yes, well, let's get this old battle wagon going. Checklist!

08:15: *We're up here dodging and ducking around trying to jockey into formation. I've never seen so many airplanes in my life. The sky is literally black with them. All I've got to say is that I'm glad they are all on my side.*

Flares of every color are shooting skyward to identify each formation. We're flying the number-three position of the first element of the low-squadron of the lead group. Easy to figure out, eh? Yep, that's your little hole right there, Rosey. The lead group fires a red-yellow flare.

09:08: *Believe it or not, we've finally got together. All these planes are an assuring sight. We've just left the coast of England. We're now over the English Channel. You know, the little strip of water that separates us from the enemy. Today, it seems extra narrow. AND HOW!*

09:30: *We've just completed the test firing of the guns. I've managed to get on my flak suit. I bet I'd weigh two hundred pounds with all this equipment I'm wearing. We're ready for anything the Jerry might throw up.*

09:47: *There she is, Holland's west coast, occupied by Nazi Germany. Just what she holds for me, I don't know. I know, frankly, I wish I was home with my mother. I don't want to be a hero—just live, that's enough for me. Buckle down, Rosey. A war's to be won. You see, I have to talk to myself. Kidding helps my morale.*

10:26: *What in the world. Over to the left front, a patch of sky is literally filled with black crust; that's flak, my first sight of the dreaded flak that I've heard so much about. This heavy flak suit that I'm wearing really feels light now. In fact, I think I'd like to have another one or two.*

11:02: *We've just turned on the IP to begin the bomb run. I've got to get this crate up there close so the bombs will fall as one ship. The bombing should be good; it's clear as a crystal, too frazzling clear. There are fighters all around. So far, no attacks.*

11:15: *We released our first bombs at the enemy at 11:06. We're circling to the left now to allow one group to make another run. Far down below, the target is one billowing mass of smoke and destruction. It looks as though it's completely demolished. I hope so. I don't want to come back here. No, sir.*

11:30: *Woe is me! We've just been attacked by enemy fighters. Those babies came within a few hundred feet of our plane and not one of my gunners shot at the fighters. Too excited to do anything but gape, and gape they did. The fighters hit our formation hard. They took two ships out of our group formation of eighteen. That's more than one-tenth of our formation in one sweep; ten attacks and no formation. Right!*

The fighters got the ship directly behind me. I looked back in time to see the big bird go into a vertical climb and spin off on one wing. I saw two chutes pop and stretch out their lazy canopies. There's eight more men in that plane. Some more chutes would be a welcome sight.

Off to the left and lower is a crippled B-17 trying to fight its way home. It has been knocked out of formation by flak or the fighters. There's about five fighters making swift passes at the ship, trying to knock it down. They look like a group of vultures gathering around, ready for the kill. It will be only a matter of seconds before she will be hurtling to earth. Dogfights can be seen everywhere. The boys have called out about three fighters they have seen go down. Smitty saw one hit the earth and burst into a billow of flames. I hope this doesn't last long. I don't crave excitement.

12:00: Whew! Will I ever be glad to get back to England. We're un-der a flak attack. Brother, this flak isn't bursting over there, it's burst-ing right here. See it! That's too close, those fellows are trying to kill us. There's a burst under the lead ship, just missed it a few feet. I think I'll join the un-army next time.

13:30: I'm taking easier breaths now. We're back out over the English Channel now, letting down. It's been rough today but I have hopes of making it back now.

21:30: Back in the barracks (believe it or not). The mission today seems just like a dream. Well, I'd say it was more like a nightmare! It's hard to believe that I'm now over here in a war where people are killing and being killed. For the first time, I fully realize that there's a war go-ing on. Yes, sir! That one trip has impressed me. Those fellows were trying to shoot me and I don't like that at all. My biggest wish is that this war was over. I'm not afraid. I just don't want to hurt anyone. Uh-huh!

I think Ivey is a little unnerved; sitting in the tail back there was just like sitting in a grandstand. I mean, he had a bird's-eye view of the whole thing. That was a lot to see at one time, and for the first time at that. I hope we have easier missions in the future. That last flak was by far the most accurate that the boys had seen in some time.

Out of the eighteen ships in the formation, fifteen had been hit by the flak; two of the ships failed to return. Kilmer, the crew behind me, had five chutes to open from his plane. That accurate flak today came from a section called Dumeur Lake. Today, we left England to Holland, France, into Germany, back across France, Holland, and return.

The action occasioned the loss of 2nd Lt. Kilmer and 1st Lt. Wilson; their crew and planes fell to the guns of a group of German fighter planes. Grady said later, "There was a dozen or so German fighters that appeared four miles above our formation. They were looping and turning and spinning, just doing acrobatic maneuvers around up there. Then they turned and dove straight down. They went well below us and made quick inverting turns and came straight up toward our belly.

"Our guys were firing for all they were worth but they couldn't slow those Germans down. In real-time, it is not like what you see in the movies. Those guys are shooting wide open and following the fighter planes all around. Our guns had so many blocks on them to keep us from shooting our own plane we could only fire in short bursts. I think the Germans knew where our blind spots were 'cause they turned all their guns loose on us from close range, and I don't know how they missed our plane. The planes on my right wing and left wing went down and the Germans disappeared. We watched parachutes open. It looked like everyone got out. That is a sad sight, watching a big bird like the B-17 fall out of control."

The crew of Lt. A. L. Kilmer consisted, on this mission, of engineer, D. F. Deitsch; right waist gunner, J. S. Alexander; radio operator, R. L. Brooks; tail gunner, A. A. Mnaisi; left waist gunner, R. G. Hicks; copilot, J. M. Hunter; navigator, W. C. Groggs; and ball-turret gunner, E. M. Gormley. Two members of the original crew—copilot, E. K. Fowler, and crew member Love—were not along for this mission. Deitsch, Alexander, Hicks, Kilmer, Hunter, and Griggs were taken prisoner, while Brooks, Mnaisi, and Gormley were listed as KIA as a result of this incident.

The plane of Lt. Wilson and his crew was aircraft 42-97440, IW-A. It was known by the nickname "Flak Rat 11." Other crews report it being hit by a single-engine German about 1100 hours just after the target. The plane of Lt. Wilson was seen to go downward from formation but under control. There were three chutes observed. Later, records show that the pilot and five crew members were taken as POWs. The right waist gunner, S/Sgt G. R. Smith, was killed and the remaining crew members were unaccounted for.

The squadron Grady flew in this mission was the low squadron. His was the only squadron hit by enemy fighter planes. The planes at the outside and low edges of the low-squadron and the outside lead and rear of the high squadron were the most exposed and most attacked by the members of the German fighter squads.

MISSION TWO

Grady did not have to wait long for his second mission. The next day—Wednesday, May 31, 1944—he was posted as one of four members of the 614th Squadron to join in the mission to Luxeuil-les-Bains, France. This was mission eighty for the group.

The 401st aircraft were led by Lt. Col. Seawell. There were fourteen B-17 from the 401st and they operated from the Low Box of the 94th CBW and used the new twelve-ship formation. There were a total of 1,029 bombers sent out with 682 fighters. The mission met few enemy fighters and encountered no flak at the target but still lost one bomber and three fighters during the course of the mission.

Grady's diary entry concerning this flight reads:

03:30: I say, chum, can they do this to me? They've just aroused me from the sack to go on another mission.

07:00: At the plane and ready to go for the second time. We kind of know what they have over there now. The target for today is a primary training field at Luxeuil, France. Just what is so important there is beyond me. They know what they're doing.

This airplane we have today has a sweet name—Betty's Revenge. I'd like to see a certain Betty I know. That's a little off the subject though, isn't it? Lucky is riding with us today. We have our own crew complete today.

08:40: We're in formation now and ready to set course. I'm number two, first element high squadron, low group. Just a fit.

09:34: *Leaving English coast.*

09:50: *We're over Belgium. It didn't take as long to cross today. We crossed the channel close to London. There's a cold front just ahead. It looks like some rough flying. I have on my flak suit and helmet. My, but they're light.*

10:20: *Smeallie and Ivey just finished firing at a fighter they said was firing at us. Those clouds back there were rather rough. All I could see was Smith, the lead ship. I mean, I've been in his lap since those fighters attacked. Talking about evasive action, I was really doing it. We've had a little scattered flak. I don't mind it as long as it's scattered but when it starts getting in the airplane with us, I don't like it worth a—*

11:58: *We've turned in the bomb run, there's no flak around but fighters are around everywhere. Most of them are friendly fighters after yesterday. They're all around us. I love those fighter pilots. If that's possible.*

12:05: *The bombs have just fallen on the target. Riep, from the ball, said it was a direct hit. I'll bet those cadets will be pissed off when they come back to their field to land.*

13:50: *We're about to leave the enemy coast. We've climbed to twenty-six thousand feet to get over the clouds. There's been a lot of contrails. I've seen pictures of vapor trails but today is the first time I've actually seen them. The trip in today was at eighteen thousand feet. A little too low for comfort.*

21:00: *Back in barracks. Today's mission wasn't too rough. We really sweated it out though. It could have been a rough baby. Friendly fighters were all over the place. Thank goodness. All the sweating we did today was almost as bad as the actual thing. The actual thing is pretty rough though. The route today was Belgium, Luxemburg, Germany, France, and back out over Belgium.*

We received our pay today; it seems like a long time since the last payday. This has been a long month. They'll all be long until I'm back with Betty. That will be the day for me. They can have the war.

June 1, Thursday, 21:00:

A very uneventful day—yes, sir. No, as you were! A very good day. I received ten letters today, can you imagine that? Mail after five weeks of anxious waiting. I mean, that was a treat. I feel like fighting a little now.

June 2, Friday, 23:30:

Another day of nothing. Lucky and I went over to Kettering this afternoon. I ordered me a pink battle jacket. Hot stuff, eh, kid? I saw the entire crew in town. Someone stole my bicycle yesterday when I went to critique. Now I'm walking.

We ate some fish and chips today. To you, that's potato chips. I'm having french-fried potatoes. They were really good. You eat the things out of a newspaper on the side of the street. I hope I didn't eat too many.

MISSION THREE

June 3, Saturday, 05:00: Neufchâtel-en-Bray, France
I'm off for another mission. This is a little later than I've been get-
ting up. Suits me okay. I'd lay in the sack all morning. I dread this mis-
sion for some unknown reason. I hope everything goes okay.

June 3, Saturday night, 21:00:
Today's mission was really a milk run. We got back to the field a lit-
tle after 1200 hours. I'm not proud though. I'd take twenty-two
missions like today.

Today's bombing was Gee Fx and PFF (radar) bombing combined.
It was completed through 10/10 cloud coverage. I don't know about the
results. The target was a nine-gun battery at Neufchâtel, France. We
were over enemy territory for about fifteen or twenty minutes. The flak
didn't get too close. There was a lot of it but it was intended for some-
one else. We flew as a group today. There was no wing formation. We
went over at twenty-one thousand feet. Some B-24s were below us at
fourteen thousand feet.

I'm really pissed off at some of the crew. Smith didn't get in till
around 0430 hours this morning. Smeallie was so sick from drinking
last night that he nearly kicked the bucket. McClung is with another
crew now. Morin is going to navigate with us.

The log from the 614th read:

"Mission 82, Major McCree led the twenty-one aircraft from the 401st BG to attack a coastal battery at Neufchâtel, France. This was in the Pas-de-Calais area and twenty-three tactical targets were attacked by PFF, obviously to draw the attention of the German high command away from the real invasion area, very successfully as it eventually turned out. Many weeks after D-Day, Hitler was still positive that the invasion would take place in the Pas-de-Calais area.

"Some flak was encountered but there were no losses and only forty-seven out of 568 bombers received some battle damage. Also, there were no crew members wounded.

"The 614th crews on this mission were:

2nd Lt. R. L. Fisette and crew
2nd Lt. W. G. Rozzell and crew
1st Lt. E. G. Owens Jr and crew
2nd Lt. La Fevor and crew
1st Lt. L. S. Bartley and crew."

Mission Four

June 4, 1944, Operational Time 0620 Hours, Massey/Palaiseau, France

For this mission, the 614th Squadron, for the first time in its history, made up a complete box, and in the same mission, the 401st supplied the planes for a complete wing with the 614th Squadron commander, Major Hinkle, flying lead for the wing.

The mission of the 401st was part of the third mission the 8th Air Force conducted on June 4. The targets were railroad bridges in the Paris area. Lt. Col. Edwin W. Brown commanded the 94th Combat Wing on this mission. The 401st made up the 5th, 6th, and 7th boxes of the formation. The target was known as "choke-point."

Bombing was visual and the results were judged to be excellent. Meager and inaccurate flak was encountered which caused a few minor holes in some of the aircraft but all returned safely to base.

The aircraft and crew of the 614th on this mission were:

1st Lt. E. G. Owens Jr. and crew
1st Lt. J. F. Risher and crew
Capt. A. H. Chapman and crew
1st Lt. W. R. Smith Jr and crew
1st Lt. J. R. Kinney and crew
1st Lt. J. A. Gruman and crew
2nd Lt. R. L. Fisette and crew

2nd Lt. C. A. Lincoln and crew
2nd Lt. F. M. Taylor and crew
2nd Lt. J. F. Lipka and crew
2nd Lt. W. G. Rozzell and crew

The diary entry for mission four of Sunday, June 4:

14:00: *This is a good time to get a fellow for a mission but that's the story. They've just called for us to be at briefing at 14:30.*

I attended chapel this morning. The service was dedicated to the men that were killed or missing in last week's raids.

June 5, Monday, 08:30:
A rather long mission, eh, kid! No, it wasn't that long; we had to land at another field further south from here. It was about thirty miles from London. The ceiling was really low. We were skimming over the tops of those hills. We got in and landed okay. We left there this morning around 08:00.

The raid yesterday was on a railroad bridge just outside the city of Paris. The mission wasn't so tough. We had flak two or three times but it wasn't so accurate. We circled around the city of Paris. The boys could see fighters strafing and dive-bombing. They seemed to be tearing everything apart. I hope they do a good job.

18:30: What's all this? Orders just came over the PA to wear gas masks, steel helmets, and pistols. Sounds like something might be in the air.

23:15: Morin and McClung have just left for briefing. C-47s are flying all over the place. They're the airborne infantry and gliders, and C-47s stationed just north of here. The barracks are wild with excitement and suspense. Everyone just knows this is the invasion. I wish I was flying. I'm really p-ed off at this sitting on the ground and all this going on.

Mission Five

June 6, 1944, was D-Day.

Colonel Harold W. Bowman did the 401st briefing this morning like this:

"Gentlemen," said Colonel Bowman, when the briefing room had quieted down, "remember the date—June 6, 1944. Remember it because your grandchildren will probably have to memorize it. This is D-Day."

The official 614th Squadron report of the D-Day activity also read:

> "So invasion day is the highlight of the 614th Squadron history, as it highlights the history of divisions, armies, and nations.
>
> "The Tannoy gave the first highlight to the base that D-Day might at long last be here. A tingle of excitement ran through the base as each man heard this announcement: 'all military personnel on the field—all military personnel on the field. You will immediately carry gas masks and helmets, you will carry a weapon with you at all times.'
>
> "That is all."

This set the rumors flying. Cliches like "this is it," "this is the big show," etc. filled the night. Cynics slightly fed up with the month-on-end false alarms, the reams of copy in the London papers about D-Day that never seemed to come off, and the dry runs that had been repeated so often scoffed at the wild talk. "Another Pas-de-Calais job," said one gunner, and many agreed.

There were more fliers in the briefing room that night than ever before, and the fight for seats was a hectic one. They filled the benches, chocked the aisles, sat on the concrete floor, and leaned against the walls.

A sound of disappointment and delight was the mixed reaction from the audience as the canvas curtain was raised to reveal the map with the routes to and from the target, marked out in colored tapes.

Some were sure it was another Pas-de-Calais job, others equally sure that it was the invasion. None of them knew until the colonel's opening remarks.

Instantly, the quiet of the room was shattered as the men awakened to the realization that the Day of Days was at hand. They yelled like wild men, they laughed, they roared, they sprang to their feet and pummeled one another.

The colonel began talking again. He told them things they knew about—how they had trained themselves for this moment, how their folks at home were banking on them, and how history would be made and a world saved if they did their jobs. He refused to cheapen the moment with melodrama or flag-waving, and so, after wishing them luck, he sat down.

After briefing was over, C-47s could be heard overhead as the towed gliders to the long-awaited rendezvous. As far as the eye could see, they stretched in clusters across the sky, with myriads of colored lights to prevent collisions.

Soon the forts began to warm up, flares were fired from the control tower. The bombers took off, one by one, down the runway—off to soften the beaches as the first seaborne troops made their epochal landings on the shores of Normandy.

The 401st flew a mission to Ver-Sur-Mer/Mont Fleury sending thirty-six B-17 to bomb the area five minutes before the troops stormed ashore. This bombing was carried out PFF. Grady was not part of the raid.

The 8th Air Force sent out 2,362 total aircraft on D-Day morning and only one of them was lost due to enemy action. At the end of the day, Lt. Col. Alison Brooks, the force leader, "commended the crews on their excellent formation maintenance and especially the tight formation over the target when bombs were released."

An indication of the importance of the invasion and the air force's commitment to it was evidenced by the presence of the commanding officer of the 8th Air Force, Lt. General Doolittle, and his deputy, Major General Earle Partridge. The generals were piloting P-38s "over the beachhead for some hours that morning."

JUNE 6, 1944, OPERATIONAL TIME 0530 HOURS TO CAEN, FRANCE

The second mission on D-Day for the 401st went to Caen, France. The 401st sent six aircraft on this mission. The six crews composed a composite box of the 94th CBW and were operating under the leadership of Captain Goodman. "Due to bad weather, the six aircraft went alone to Caen, but due to solid undercast, they were unable to find their target and returned with their bombs.

"Some flak was met as the group passed over the Channel Islands, which was meager but fairly accurate."

The 614th Squadron put up two aircraft for this mission:

1st Lt. R. H. Kaufman and crew
2nd Lt. W. G. Rozzell and crew

June 6, Tuesday, 03:30:
Say, it does look like something is happening and I'm not going to sit on the ground after all. They've come for us to go to briefing. Morin is riding with another crew.
13:30: *D-DAY AT LAST—INVASION OF FRENCH COAST*

I've just returned from a raid to Caen, France. We flew right over the top of the invasion. The clouds covered the entire affair. That was so bad, not getting to see it. The target was a railroad and overrunning bridge that supply German troops. We didn't get to bomb the target because of the clouds.

The first raid dropped their bombs. Boy, I wish we had dropped those babies. Those boys need all the help we can possibly muster out for them. I'm ready to fly until I drop. Any altitude or any time we've had few reports.

P-38s, P-47s, C-47s are grouping under the clouds. C-47s did drop those paratroopers and gliders last night. I thought there was something stirring. You could almost feel it in the air. We've been waiting for this and here it is. Yep, the big day of the ETO. I'm glad that it's finally arrived. There's going to be many a good man killed today. Blessing on them.

Grady's mission on D-Day was officially number eighty-five for the 401st. The records state:

> *"The second 401st mission on D-Day went to Caen when six aircraft from the group, under the leadership of Captain Goodman, took the lead of the 94th CBW composite box. Due to solid undercast sky, the six aircraft went alone to Caen but they were unable to find their target and returned with their bombs."*

Back home in Center Post, Georgia, the word of the invasion reached the household of Betty, her mother, Mamie, and father, Carlos, by radio. Carlos was in his cotton field chopping weeds. Betty went to tell him the news and take him some water.

Carlos was a veteran of the first World War and recipient of two Purple Hearts. When Betty told him of the invasion, Carlos became overwhelmed emotionally and Betty says simply, he "fell to the ground and cried."

Carlos was concerned about his son-in-law Grady but an additional worry was his son, Joel Clayton Thomas, who was now of draft age. Joel was called and inducted into active service on July 11, 1944. The son was destined to fight in some of the same European fields on which his father, Carlos, had done battle. He also received two Purple Hearts.

MISSION SIX

"The 614th Squadron was the lead of the high box which bombed a tactical target by PFF through 10/10 cloud at Falaise, France. This was a target south of the invasion area and a rail and transportation point leading into the area behind the German troops. Blocking these points allowed the ground-strafing aircraft and fighter-bombers of the RAF and the USAAF to devastate the German reinforcements trying to reach the invasion areas.

"Because of a malfunction in the GH equipment, two runs had to be made over the target. There was some meager and inaccurate flak but none of the group aircraft was damaged in any way."

The 614th crew flying in this mission were:

1st Lt. R. H. Kaufman and crew
1st Lt. J. R. Kenney and crew
1st Lt. F. W. Taylor and crew
1st Lt. J. F. Risher and crew
2nd Lt. W. G. Rozzell and crew

June 7, Wednesday, 21:30:
We went on another invasion mission today. We raided the middle

143

of the town of Falaise, France. It was a new type of Gee bombing through clouds. I hope they did some good. They were trying to tear up the through highways coming through the middle of town. There's going to be hundreds of innocent civilians meeting their destiny, but this is war, I suspect.

Fowler, my new bombardier, was navigating today. We flew number three in the lead squadron. We carried a camera, and at the arrival over the English coast, we were told to peel off and bring the camera back home.

I came to find out that Fowler didn't even have a map of the way home. He gave me a heading to fly. I flew the heading of the big formation and bracketed it to a fine degree. I flew radio compass in when we got close to the field. I went in and bitched to Maj. Garland when we got back. Morin is slated to ride with us tomorrow. We saw a few ships today. This mission gave us the Air Medal.

MISSION SEVEN

JUNE 8, 1944, OPERATIONAL TIME 0500 HOURS TO MANTES, FRANCE

June 8, Thursday, 22:00:

00:30: *Rather early for briefing but this is it.*

21:00: *Whew, what a screwed-up day. Just as we were getting ready to taxi out, the guy in front of us ran off the perimeter and got stuck in the mud. We waited a while for him to get out but to no avail. At the last moment, they took my crew to a spare airplane.*

When we got there, they had to change the starter. When we finally got started, we were one and a half hours late. We made a beeline for the coast but never did find our formation. We joined another formation and went on over to bomb at Mantes Cassncourt, France, a small city just north of Paris.

The formation was really a scary one. I wasn't the only stranger in the bunch. The wingman had a Block A and then there were two B-24s off to the right. There were five fields represented in the box.

When we got back, we found all our ships returned before the raid. We were the only crew that got a mission today. We saw the invasion today. Millions of little crafts in the harbor. Hundreds of gliders were where they landed and were left. I hope they go right on into Berlin.

June 9, Friday, 21:30:

We were slated to fly today but there was no mission. This weather around here is terrible; I wish it would clear up. We can do those boys a lot of good over there.

It seems like everyone on the field knows about our flying with another formation yesterday. I'm taking a lot of ribbing about joining up with a B-24 outfit. I left my jacket with Harry Hall to get it painted today. I'm going to name my ship "Rosie's Sweat Box."

We didn't get to fly our own plane yesterday. The one we flew was a wreck. The tail wheel's sheer pin sheered and we went out through the middle of the field when we landed. I flew a ship the other day that had been hit eighty times by flak on the Oschersleben Raid (my first). I suspect we were really lucky not to get hit at all.

They're moving fighters up fast on the invasion front. I'm expecting them to tear into us anytime now. We're on loading for tomorrow. I hope we can make a successful mission.

Smith and Crane left today. They completed their thirty missions and are going home. Lucky boys.

MISSION EIGHT

JUNE 11, 1944, OPERATIONAL TIME 0635 HOURS TO
BERNAY, FRANCE

This was the eighth mission for the 401st in the month of
June. The target was an airfield at Bernay/Saint-Martin, France.
There were "twenty-one aircraft from the group, under the
command of Major Leon Stann." The planes made up the low
box of the 94th CBW, and though it was scheduled to be a visual
bombing run, the bombs were released on the Gee-H, which was
run on the second trip over the target.

This was one of the rare occasions when no enemy opposition
was encountered, no flak, no enemy aircraft.

The 614th Squadron crews participating:

1st Lt. E. G. Owens Jr. and crew
2nd Lt. W. G. Rozzell and crew
2nd Lt. R. L. Fisette and crew
1st Lt. L. S. Bartley and crew
1st Lt. J. R. Kenney and crew
1st Lt. G. L. La Fevor and crew

June 10, Saturday, 21:00:
Brother, this was the day for me. Yep, a day of days, a day of eases,
of solid comfort. A day of nothing but sack, sack!

147

23:30: *Looks as though I talked too soon—we've been alerted for a mission. That means no sleep at all tonight.*

June 11, Sunday, 22:00:
Boy, this was a screwed-up affair today. The target was an airfield southwest of Bernay, France. We carried sixteen 250-pound GP bombs. Two of the ships carried delayed fuse bombs. The bombing altitude today was nineteen thousand feet, a little too low for a lumbering box like this fort. Clouds covered the target on the first run so we went around on a cross-country trip. The bomb-bay doors would not come up electrically so I had Smeallie crank them up.

After what seemed an eternity, we came back for a second run on the target. This time our bomb-bay doors wouldn't come down. So I asked Smeallie to crank them down. He told me to let someone else crank them down, that his arm was about to drop off. Whew, did that burn me up. Here we are seconds to bombs away and he pulls a trick like that.

I did wrong by asking Burnett to come up and crank instead of making Smeallie go ahead and get them down. I think Smeallie was afraid to crank them. While Burnett was coming up, Fowler told me that we could just salvo the bombs and bomb-bay doors. We were too close to the target to crank them down. So I decided to let him salvo. We came in on the approach without bomb-bay doors.

MISSION NINE

JUNE 12, 1944, OPERATIONAL TIME 0550 HOURS TO VITRY-EN-ARTOIS, FRANCE

This was one of the target missions launched by the 8th Air Force. The mission of June 12 placed 1,442 B-17s and B-24s and 988 fighters in the skies of northern France. Eight bombers and sixteen fighters were lost, with the Luftwaffe up in strength for the first time since the Allies had landed in Normandy. Well over two hundred bombers returned to their bases with battle damage, with many men killed and injured.

The 401st put up thirty-six aircraft with Lt. Col. B. K. Voorhees as the group leader. Two of the boxes of aircraft bombed successfully but the third one was just about to release its bombs when another group of aircraft passed under it.

The 614th Squadron members on the mission:

1st Lt. E. G. Owens Jr. and crew
2nd Lt. F. M. Taylor and crew
1st Lt. J. P. Risher and crew
1st Lt. J. R. Kenney and crew
2nd Lt. G. L. La Fevor and crew
1st Lt. L. S. Bartley and crew
2nd Lt. G. A. Filemyr and crew
2nd Lt. W. G. Rozzell and crew
Lead crew:
Capt. A. H. Chapman, pilot

Lt. Col. B. K. Voorhees, copilot and air commander
Capt. C.M. Smith, navigator
Major J. Pickoff, bombardier
T/Sgt R.B. Pyle, radio
T/Sgt G.S Wilson, top turret and engineer
1st Lt. R.W Harger, tail gunner and observer
S/Sgt B.J. Spatilson, ball turret
Col. E.P Maschmeyer, left waist gunner
S/Sgt M. G. Brennen, right waist gunner

June 12, Monday, 00:30:
This can't go on forever. They've just got me out of bed for another mission. I hadn't gone sound asleep. This makes two successive nights with no sleep.

22:00: *Needless to say, I'm rather pooped tonight. We had better results with our bombing today than we've been having the last two or three missions. The target was an airfield at Vitry airport. We carried thirty-four 100-pound high-explosive bombs today.*

We went in over Holland, across Belgium, into France. There was flak all along the line. Some of it was very accurate. The good part— they didn't shoot at us today. They were too busy shooting at the other ships. Thank goodness! We turned on the bomb run, bombs away, direct hit, and off on our way home.

I made some pictures of the flak and formation today. There was a big red burst in front of us today. I thought it was a red burst of flak but I was told it was a B-17 exploding.

We certainly had a bad accident today. Some of the boys were removing a fragmentation bomb and the thing exploded. The little twenty-three-pound bomb killed five men and wounded twelve others. They had arms and legs thrown everywhere. They say it was a bloody sight. I saw the plane. It's a wreck.

The surviving records from the accident stated that it was

actually responsible for the death of six men. Eleven members of the Ordnance and Armament sections sustained injuries of varying severity. It occurred while the men were unloading some fragmentation bombs from an aircraft and dropped one of them.

The men who were killed were:

Sgt. R. T. Humphry
Cpl. A. Milunie
Cpl. L. B. Weber
Pfc. J. H. Oliver
T/Sgt. J. F. Bradsher
Sgt. A. B. Hecht Jr.

For the first time since I've had my crew, I chewed ass this morning. After yesterday's occurrence, I was still plenty p-ed. I told the boys the old stuff would have to cease. I wasn't satisfied with their attitude and we'd have to have a little more work and less bitching. I believe it did some good.

June 12, Tuesday, 24:00:
This is one hell of a time to be getting up. They called at 23:30. Brother, this is the third straight night that I haven't slept. This old— gets old.

03:30: *Have you ever seen a happy lad? Well, here's one. They scrubbed the mission, going to hit the sack and never get up.*

20:00: *This day has been okay. Just screwed around doing nothing. We practiced ditching this afternoon and went in to see Maj. Garland about Henderson. He's been getting sick and going to sleep on missions.*

A new crew came in today. Boy, I know exactly how they feel. I was new a month ago. I sure don't feel like a recruit now. I get a big kick out of their expressions. I showed them the community drawer where we keep the belongings of the crews who go down. I mean, they really gaped. To make it worse, when we went over to supply, they had a bunch of boxes they were sending home for fellows MIA (missing in action).

Mission Ten

Colonel Bowman led sixty B-17s from the 401st to attack the famous Le Bourget airfield, which was used as a night-fighter base, supply and repair depot, and had large transport facilities. It was an important German Air Force operational base. The 614th put up fourteen aircraft of the sixty furnished by the group. Colonel Bowman led the 1st Division of 502 aircraft on one assigned separate MPIs (the main target of bomb impact) and everyone was a "shack" (direct hit). Major Kinkle led the high box with Capt. C. M. Smith as navigator and Lt. G. H. B. Brairton as bombardier.

Moderate, accurate flak was encountered at the target and one fighter attack occurred near the I.P. 2nd Lt. R. H. Schroeder of the 615th Squadron was lost on this occasion.

Crew of the 614th on this mission:

1st Lt. E. G. Owens Jr and crew
1st Lt. R. L. Fisette and crew
Capt. A. H. Chapman and crew
1st Lt. R. H. Kaufman and crew
1st Lt. J. F. Lipka and crew
1st Lt. J. F. Risher and crew
2nd Lt. G. A. Filemyr and crew
2nd Lt. T. D. Carroll and crew

1st Lt. L. S. Bartley and crew
1st Lt. J. A. Gruman and crew
1st Lt. F. M. Taylor and crew
1st Lt. C. A. Lincoln and crew
2nd Lt. W. G. Rozzell and crew
1st Lt. G. L La Fevor and crew

June 14, Wednesday, 00:30:
Here we go again. I don't feel so bad tonight though. I've had a little sleep in the last twenty-four hours.

22:00: *I say, old man, it was rough and rugged today. The target was the Le Bourget Airport in Paris, France. It was here that Lindberg landed on his Transatlantic flight. He can thank his lucky stars that he was not held over there today. Exactly 1,276,000 pounds of bombs fell there today. We carried eighteen 250-pound GPs. We flew tail-end Charlie today.*

Our field put up sixty airplanes today, which were formed into five 12-ship boxes. We had a box from Glatton to give us two wings from this field. We led the 1st Division on the mission today. Col. Bowman led the lead group. We flew in the high box. Flak started popping shortly after we started on the run, and I mean to tell you, it was not wasted at all.

Just as we were turning on the IP, six Me-109s came in from the nose, dived under us, and took a ship out of the low box. It was Schroeder, a classmate of mine at Hendricks. It was his second mission. He was a personal hometown friend of Jr. Kaufman, one of the first pilots here in my barracks. It was really a tough break.

We made the run okay and started for home. Out of our five groups, we had five shacks, a perfect score for the 401st. Glatton, the extra group in our second wing, had a little misfortune. A burst of flak hit the lead ship, exploding it and getting the two wing ships. That was three ships at once. Can't stand much of that.

I thought Schroder's plane was going to hit us when it was knocked out. He came up at us in a fighting, uncontrollable climb, and at the

154

last moment, he pulled straight up and into a spin. Two chutes came out as the big ship spun earthward.

Our return to base was uneventful.

There was a little event that caused a lot of comment this morning. As two of the boys (McClung and Morin) left this morning to go to breakfast, they ran across a soldier and his English girl lying in the bushes enjoying one of nature's oldest and most intimate relationships.

June 15, Thursday, 21:00:

Another good day of sack time. I went over to see the jacket I'm having painted by Harry Hall. He is doing a nice job.

We're having stinky weather here; I don't have much hopes of a mission tomorrow. I received six letters today. I haven't written for three days.

June 16, Friday, 22:00:

We were gotten up this morning at 0415 hours to go on a mission. After we had been briefed and at the airplane and ready to start engines, the mission was scrubbed. The mission today was deep into France. It was an airfield that they know nothing about. They didn't even know if there was a field there or not.

The boys are having a little party tonight. They have a case of soda, two bottles of rum, a bottle of Three Feathers. I hope my boys don't go for it too strong. I'm the biggest sucker that ever came from Tennessee if they fly with me tomorrow.

June 17, Saturday, 00:30:

What a rip-roaring time we've been having tonight. This barrack has really been a madhouse. Nearly everyone in here is drunk, and here we are, going to briefing for an operational mission. Morin and McClung are especially feeling good. The fellows have been initiating the new crew tonight. They've really made 'em live hard. They've just finished upsetting Lt. Perry's bed. They picked on him mostly tonight. Bottles are everywhere. In general, it's just a mad scramble.

21:30: The mission was scrubbed this morning. It's a good thing too. Too many of the fellows had been drinking. That's no good. Smith and Smeallie got in late last night; I am certainly disgusted. That's the second time for Smith and the last time Smeallie was sick from drinking. I have just finished having a little talk with them. Smith and Smeallie are restricted for a week. None of the boys are going to town the night before we are scheduled for a mission.

I feel all out of place tonight. I'm lonely, sad, and blue.

The nearby towns of Deenthorpe, Benefield, and Weldon played a vital role in the social life of the soldiers of the 401st. The base had a PX and officers club and enlisted club but they lacked the diversion, which even the most remote prospect of contact with a member of the fairer sex provided. There were not sufficient single females in the neighborhood to meet the demands but there were women there and that was sufficient to fuel the imagination of men so far from home.

On the Weldon road just off the northeast boundary of the base and a mile or so from Lower Benefield was the Wheatsheaf Inn. It was a short walk or bike ride from any part of the airfield and a popular hangout. We were fortunate to visit the inn in '07 and find some folk who had lived there during the time of the 401st tenure.

One of the first people we encountered was a lady employed at the Wheatsheaf Inn. She was very easy to talk to about the war and the role the soldiers played in the community. The men were nearly universally loved by the villagers. The Americans took on the cause of all the children. They got very close and the sentiment was returned. The people from the village watched the planes leaving on missions each morning and would be back at the end of the runway to count the returning planes.

The locals had friends at all levels on the base, and by knowing how many pounds of bombs the planes were carrying compared to how much gas was on board, they knew what time to expect them to return. There was much secrecy about the target of an individual raid but the men who fueled and armed the planes with bombs could let the interested villagers know how long their fliers would be away without compromising any military objectives.

The mother of our friend from the Wheatsheaf Inn had been close to Col. Bowman. The mother had done the laundry for the colonel and kept in touch with him after the war. She had received a personal Christmas card each year until her death.

She also shared a story concerning her sister. The sister had a terrier dog. The dog loved to stay on the base. One of the crews adopted the dog as a mascot and got so attached they would not fly a mission without the dog. As too many of these stories go, one of the crew members accidentally ran over and killed the dog.

Christmas is not an easy time so far from home. The members of the 401st, on December 24, 1943, entertained 650 English children in the mess hall with plenty to eat and gifts for each child. The number of children seems a little overstated until you realize the number of children sent out of the city of London to live with rural relatives when the German bombing attacks were so deadly in that town. It is hard to tell whether the children or the soldiers enjoyed the party most.

The softball team of the 401st won the 1st Division summer tourney. I asked Grady about the sports, which were likely to be played on base. Grady was a baseball player of note and, in later times, a successful coach of softball for both men and women. He was known to invest a lot of time in the pursuit of a good game, much less a good season. He assured me he did not know of any sports played at Deenethorpe. After more prodding, he further assured me he did not know where the officers club was nor had he been to the Wheatsheaf Inn or even the PX. He said, "The air force got their full service out of me." I think he was correct.

MISSION ELEVEN

The 8th Air Force now turned its attention back to the German homelands "with a force of 1,380 8th Air Force bombers and 817 fighters attacking oil refineries in Hamburg, Moosburg, and Bremen, the 2nd Air Division going after the Luftwaffe control centers at Fassberg and Stade. Due to weather closing in, attacks were made by PFF on secondary targets and targets of opportunity.

"Major D. E. Silver led the forty aircraft from the group to form the 94th 'A' Combat Wing. The accuracy of the bombing could not be confirmed but clouds of black smoke were seen raising to about sixteen thousand feet and the area continued to burn for some days afterward.

"No enemy aircraft were seen but flak was moderate to intense at the target area, causing some battle damage to aircraft from the group, but they all returned to Deenethorpe."

Aircraft from 614th on this mission included:

2nd Lt. W. G. Rozzell and crew
1st Lt. R. H. Kaufman and crew
2nd Lt. T. D. Carroll and crew
1st Lt. J. F. Risher and crew
1st Lt. R. L. Fisette and crew
1st Lt. J. F. Lipka and crew

2nd Lt. G. A. Filemyer and crew
1st Lt. F. M. Taylor and crew
1st Lt. L. S. Bartley and crew

June 18, Sunday, 01:30:
Off to briefing again — won't they ever slow down?
22:00: *Today's mission was a little different from some of the milk runs we've had. Hamburg, Germany, was the target. We were gunning for the oil refineries around the docks. Clouds covered the target, almost 10/10s. We bombed PFF. I don't know about the results. The flak was thick as all get out. How we got through with no hits is beyond me. We made it through and that's good enough for me. That was an eight-hour haul today. A long time to fight a B-17 aircraft.*

We had a little incident happen when we were parking today. We taxied into the dispersal area, applied the brakes, but the plane just kept right on rolling. I looked and had no hydraulic pressure. I reached down and put on the manual pump and she stopped okay. It was a good thing that there were no planes immediately ahead of us. If there had been, it would be minus a tail and so would Rosey.

I've found out something that really helps my morale. We have to fly thirty-five missions instead of thirty. When we left home, we had twenty-five missions to go before we rotated home to the states. Now we've flown eleven and still have exactly twenty-four more to go. Not much gain. Nothing fair in the army!

MISSION TWELVE

June 19, Monday, 00:30:

I wish they would leave me in the sack for one morning.

22:00: Brother, I'll live a long time before I forget this day. The mission was to Bordeaux, France. We climbed in the haze and stratus clouds up to twenty-eight thousand feet before we actually broke through. About half of the formation straggled and four of our planes didn't even make it through the clouds. That was rough going. After a little while, we were back in wing formation and everything went along okay.

On the way to the target, Filmer suddenly left the formation and started a rapid, spinning descent. When he was only a few thousand feet from the formation his plane blew to bits.

We descended all the way to the target and started our bomb run at twenty thousand feet. We were about halfway down the bomb run and all Hell started popping loose. We snaked right on through and then four big bursts exploded almost on our ship. The concussion nearly blew us sky-high. The roaring sounded more like thunder, which was enough to keep a fellow from sleeping for months. I could hear flak slapping the ship like hail against a tin roof and then the thing we'd been waiting for—bombs away and a steep turn to get our tight poop holes out of there.

We turned to the right, out by the way of the Bay of Biscay, across

France, and home. On the way back, we had to climb to 31,800 feet to get over the soup. Smeallie had to crank the bomb-bay doors up. The controls had been shot away. There was one bomb left hanging in the bomb bay so we just put the safety pin back in it and brought it back home with us. I figure that we kill enough innocent French people without kicking aimless bombs out.

About five minutes after we'd turned from the target, Bralley CTG called up and said he had some plexiglass in his rear end. He walked back to the radio room and Burnett fixed him up with some bandages. He came up to the front and stayed there for the rest of the way home.

Lucky and Burnett thought we had a flat tire. They had heard a hissing sound which turned out to be an oxygen bottle. When we came back and peeled, I went around and landed last in the formation for fear of blocking the runway with a flat tire. We landed okay and I called the ambulance for Bralley.

Looking our ship over, I've decided that we're about the luckiest crew on God's earth to be back at the field. We could have easily lost one or all of our engines. Morin, Bralley, and Burnett are extremely lucky to be here. A piece of flak burst the side window and shattered the side of the left nose gun. Another piece came right down by my head and all the way through the nose. A piece came right through and out the plexiglass nose. A piece hit Bralley in the rear and put a lot of plexiglass in his seat. His flying suit's tail-end looked like a bulldog had had a hold of him.

A piece of flak hit Burnett's gun and tore the side off it; it almost ripped it from the upper hatch. Bralley gave me a piece of flak that came from the seat of his pants. We had a hole through number one gas tank, a large hole through the cowling, and into the cy. head of number two engine. Number three engine had the supercharger hit and number four engine had a burst through the induction system.

Needless to say, our plane is in the Subdepot and will be for some time. My entire crew almost quit on me today. After the bomb run on the way back though, they were ready to fly again tomorrow. I found out that they had flak school there at the target. Brother, the instructors were schooling us. I went to see Capt. Hardesty, flight surgeon, tonight. He *gave me some sleeping pills for the boys when we need them. We're nervous and scared.*

This is the worksheet for Rosie's Sweat Box after mission twelve.

450th Sub Depot, AAF Station 128, U. S. Army.

The following is the work schedule on A/C 42-97872

1. Replace Bombardier's sighting panel.
2. Repair two holes in plexi-glass nose
3. Replace left beam gun window.
4. Replace damaged oxygen bottle below top turret
5. Replace #3 supercharger
6. Replace #4 right flap screw retaining block
7. Remove right outboard panel.
8. Replace damaged tokios.
9. Replace panel when finsihed.
10. Replace #4 cylinder, #2 engine.
11. Clean up two holes in chin turret tub.
12. Repair hole, left side of fuselage below astrodome.
13. Repair hole, left side of fuselage at leading edge of wing.
14. Repair hole forward of right bombay door.
15. Repair hole in right bombay door.
16. Repair three holes in left bombay door.
17. Repair two holes in bottom of Blk. #4.
18. Repair one hole in bottom of Blk. #5.
19. Repair hole in left wing root fairing trl. edge.
20. Repair crack, at left of ball turret.
21. Repair hole on left side of radi hatch.
22. Repair hole through radio hatch frame.
23. Repair hole at bottom of fuselage below, waist window.
24. Repair sheet metal damage on left elevator.
25. Repair hole in left side of vertical fin fairing.
26. Repair hole at top of vertical fin above "S".
27. Repair hole in bottom of tail gun emplacement.
28. Repair twoholes in right side of fuselge in "W".
29. Repair hole in stainless steel fwd. #3 spchg.
30. Repair two holes on left side of right wheel well.
31. Repair hole in rear blkhead of right wheel well.
32. Repair hole in rightwing oil cooler door.
33. Repair hole, lef t side of #4 nacelle.
34. Repair hole in #4 intercooler air duct.
35. Repair hole, bottom of right wing aft of outbd flap control door.
36. Repair hole and rib at flap control door aft of #4 nacelle.
37. Repair hole aft #3 feeder, splice broken rib and stiffener.
38. Repair hole and stiffner aft of #3 nacelle.
39. Rapair two skin, rib and corrugation holes, on bottom of right outbd panel.
40. Repair hole, lower right section #2 ring cowl.
41. Repair hole, leading edge left wing at #2 oil cooler.
42. Repair hole in trailing edge left wing at tank vents.
43. Repair hole in fairing on Sta. 19, left wing.
44. Repair hole, bottom of left wing outboard of #1.
45. Repair three holes in trailing edge of right wing.
46. Repair hole in top of leading edge right wing between nacelles.
47. Repair hole in top of trailing edge, left wing.
48. Repair holes in left side of Blk. 1B, 2 and 2A.
49. Repair two holes aft of left beam gun window.
50. Repair R&R fabric hole in left elevator.
51. Repair fabric hole in rudder.
52. Repair wires broken on left side of Blk #2.

Mission Thirteen

June 20, Tuesday, 01:30:

Won't this ever end? If we go today it will be number thirteen, or
"12A" as the boys like to call it. It is real funny as to how superstitious
a fellow gets over here. I wouldn't fly without the little testament or the
little colorful ball that Betty gave me. Nearly every fellow has one of his
own lucky charms, ranging from Catholic prayers to colorful bright
ties. I'm as drunk as all get out this morning from that sleeping pill. I'll
try another one tonight.

21:30: Big Thirteen finished. We went back to Hamburg again today. The weather was ideal, and did the bombardiers take advantage of
it. When we left, old Hamburg was a mass of flame and smoke. More
boiled Germans. That's the most smoke and flame I ever hope to see.
Imagine tons and tons of high explosives and incendiaries falling into a
square mile of oil refineries. On the left page is a picture of the bomb
damage just shortly after we hit. When we left, the sun was three times
as high. Good work!

Incidentally, the Germans took full advantage of the clear weather to
throw up their flak. We were fortunate today. All they did was knock a
large hole through the plexiglass of the top turret and a few scattered
holes in the wings. I found out that my ship had a little over fifty holes
in it from Bordeaux. It's in the subdepot now getting all fixed up. They
had the wings off, putting in some new gas tanks.

Bralley will be in the hospital for up to fifty days; I think he'll be out a little sooner though. Bralley wanted to get his fingertip shot so he could get the Purple Heart. They missed his finger a little bit but he has his Purple Heart. We have twenty more missions. I will be glad when they are finished and how!

These sleeping pills are wonderful things. I was having a wonderful time at breakfast and briefing this morning. It wore off out at the airplane and I was still the same frazzle. If you've ever seen anyone with their ass dragging, here he is.

The 614th history said of the mission: "Back to Hamburg where additional dock and industrial installations were bombed. Major Hinkle, who received the DFC for this mission, led with Captain Cammack, and strike photos showed that the job was well done. The thirty-eight aircraft of the group furnished the high box of the 94th CBQW 'A' and 'B' formations.

"No enemy fighters were seen, but the flak in the target area was described as intense and very accurate. This can be seen by the fact that, of the 1,448 aircraft over Germany that morning, forty-nine went missing in action and 842 returned with battle damage. On the aircraft that returned, twelve of the crew members were dead, forty-four wounded. A very hard battle had been fought in the skies of Germany that June morning."

The 614th crews who battled their way to Hamburg on this mission were:

2nd Lt. W. G. Rozzell and crew
2nd Lt. T. D. Carroll and crew
1st Lt. G. L. La Fevor and crew
1st Lt. C. A. Lincoln and crew
1st Lt. F. M. Taylor and crew
1st Lt. L. S. Bartley and crew
1st Lt. R. L. Fisette and crew
1st Lt. J. F. Fisher and crew
Capt. V. K. Cammack and crew

Mission Fourteen

June 21, Wednesday, 00:30:
They can't keep this up forever. I can't take it much longer.

22:00: *We hit Big B today. Talking about some boys sweating out a mission we did. We were expecting everything in the book to be thrown at us today. Well, they saved the covers. In the after-briefing service this morning, Chaplain Fellows read the scripture that says, "The Lord shall preserve thy going in and thy coming out." I believe that.*

We went up and around onto Berlin. The contrails were rough. By some means, we managed to stay together and threw our bombs all over Berlin, and we left and fast. They assign us some military target in Berlin but they always end up bombing the important shoe and jewelry stores in the heart of the city. Rough on civilians, ain't it?

Lt. Perry, one of the new bombardiers, rode with us today for his first mission. Rather rough for the first time. We went through without the first scratch today. Big B is twenty square miles of flak. If they ever get your number, it's just curtains.

I saw a good fight today. Three fighters were shot down in about a minute or less. They seemed to disintegrate. One of them started cart-wheeling and broke into pieces and fluttered to earth in three or four pieces. I saw some propaganda sheets floating down today. An easy way to win a war. Quite effective, I think.

The boys said there was 10/10 coverage of flak at the target today. I think the mission was a retaliation for the flying bombs that the Germans have been sending over on London the past few days. Personally, I'd rather be in London than Berlin. All that flak coming back down is enough without even considering those bombs.

This is one of the pins from the bomb load Grady dropped onto Berlin. Grady mailed it to his father with the note, "#14 Big B. How about that. Big Promise? I did it."

Before he left to start his combat mission, Grady had told his father, Frank, he was going to bomb Berlin. Frank had told him that if he did "I'll take care of you for life."

When he was released from active duty, Grady moved back to Chattanooga to work with Frank until he could finish his education. As he had no other place to live, he and Betty moved into the Rozzell residence in East Lake. As part of the big promise to care for him, Grady figured he would at least have a place to live until he found a new residence. As Grady told me about the situation, "The second week I was there, he asked me for rent."

Mission Fifteen

June 22:

What in the world, I'm no superman. I'm shot.

21:00: *Today's mission was about a dream. We bombed in the Dunkirk area directly across the channel. The only thing wrong with the mission was the long drawn-out bomb run. The bomb-bay doors were dropped all the time we were over land. Hinkle led today. They overshot the target going in and got another one coming out. I think it was an airport. The whole coast is one big bomb crater. I'll take all my missions over there. I love that, practically no flak. Ah, boy!*

This makes about fifteen missions in twenty-four days. Too many. I think we'll get a rest tomorrow. I know I can't fly much more. I'm just about done for. I bet my mother wouldn't know me. I'm going to take another sleeping pill and hit the sack. They've kept me alive the last few days. I think Germany is ready to quit bombing London with their flying bombs if we leave Berlin alone. Do you think we'll agree to that? I don't either. Let's sack it.

June 23, Friday, 21:30:

I knew that sooner or later they'd give us a day off. That was it and was it sweet. I went down to S-2 and talked to Lt. Don Sotherland a little while this afternoon. He gave me some pictures of flak and formations. I haven't seen enough of it; I want some pictures, am I mad?

June 24–26, Grady Took Leave to London.
June 24, 14:30:
Believe it or not, I'm going out on a pass. Yeh, bet your life a —— pass. I think we'll go to London.

June 26, Monday, 23:00:
We have just returned from a couple of days in London. Frankly, I don't know if I'll go back or not. It's bad enough to bomb but to be bombed is still worse. At least we know where our bombs are going to fall. Doodle Bugs are falling haphazardly.

We arrived in London Saturday evening around 19:00. We boarded a subway and went with the aid of two girls, we were able to find a hotel. It was rather hard to get rid of the two girls.

Morin and I stayed inside the hotel and sent poor old Lucky out to tell the girls we were going to get some rest. Our hotel was the Regent Palace, a very nice hotel, I must say. I'll never forget that downy pillow. The softest sack that this worn-out skeleton ever laid on.

We spent the evening looking here and yon. Morin was feeling pretty good at dinner tonight. He was trying to get a bucktoothed blonde waitress to come up to his room. If he'd been sober at all he wouldn't have spoken to her.

I got a kick out of the newspaper men on the street. They'd yell, "Papers, papers," and then a lowered voice would say, "Condoms, condoms."

I attended the Sunday morning service at Westminster Abbey. Such a quaint and ancient place. Everything had a death-like appearance. Tombs were in all the walls. Statues and monuments to the dead. Tomb of the unknown soldier. The service was something special. All the bishops, priests, or whatever you call the speakers, were loudly crowded around. I don't know exactly what took place. They sang some songs that I had never heard. They prayed in a high song-like pitch. After the service, they had communion. The wine was real strong and tingly. I'd like to have some of it to drink after a mission.

After the service, the speakers and their attendants filed from the platform carrying torches, banners, and all kinds of things, like poles. The service seemed medieval.

Sunday afternoon we hired a taxi and went to see where some of the bombs had fallen Saturday night. Poor old Lucky nearly went into hysterics Saturday night. He could hardly let me sleep. He'd hear one of the bombs coming and then he'd hear the motor cut out. Then he'd kick me and say, "Listen, Rosey, and you'll hear a bomb drop." A few seconds later a loud explosion would occur, doors would bang and windows would shake. We saw the closest bomb hit which was a few blocks away at the Victoria train station. That two-thousand-pound airplane certainly does its share of destruction when it hits. They sound somewhat like a CE fighter plane when they dive overhead.

Sunday afternoon we went to the big PX over on Oxford Circle but it was closed for inventory. We rode around a little in a taxi seeing Buckingham Palace, Parliament, and some other places. Lucky and I had a lot of fun gabbing with the chambermaid there on the sixth floor. Her name was Hannah Hngland from Ireland. She had worked there at the hotel for two years.

We came in late at the field tonight. I hope nothing is said about it. We finally got over to the PX in London.

June 27, Tuesday, 21:00:

Say, this will never do. Rozzell is a 1st Lt.

Major Hinkle called me over and started chewing me out about a vulgar picture I had on my ship. Then he wanted to know where I'd been the last two days. I didn't know what was up. After talking for about five minutes, he finally told me I could put on the silver bar. Suits me okay.

We had another scrubbed mission today. Kaufman really had a happy jag on last night. He had been over at the celebration of 401st one-hundredth mission. Kaufman rarely ever drinks but he was happy tonight. He was throwing chairs here and yon, pulling everyone's bedding off, and finally ended up vomiting in it. He said his buddy Schultz had gotten him drunk. He did a good part of it.

June 28, Wednesday, 22:00:

Another wonderful day of sack. A mission left the field this morning but did not return because our field was closed by clouds. It has been raining all day. I've written several letters tonight. I should, though I haven't written in a week.

June 29, Thursday, 22:00:

Rested again today. I went to the infirmary with Zimmer, our photographer, in a jeep. We had a good time speeding along. I listened to some good stories tonight. One of the new officers was telling about a disheartening experience he had just before he left the states. He caught the "clap" from his wife. Could you think of anything worse? Of course, he has a divorce now. Can't blame him at all.

July 4, Tuesday, 20:00:

Rozzell also ran. We pulled our first abortion this morning. This was the first time we had flown our ship, Rosie's Sweat Box, since she came out of the subdepot from our twelfth mission.

We took off and were climbing to an altitude for assembly when number four engine went haywire. The oil pressure went up. Cyl. head temperature soared and oil started spurting from the cowling. We feathered it and came on back down. After descending, we found the field almost covered with an eight hundred-foot haze. Somehow we managed to get her over the end of the long runway and set her down about half of its length.

It isn't too much fun landing through haze with a full bomb load, full gas load, and an outboard engine feathered. I'm just glad it was a long runway. I made some pictures of the plane. I'm afraid we won't be flying her for another few days now. They're changing engines.

July 5, Wednesday, 21:00:

Didn't do much today. We tested the AFCE in the lead plane for tomorrow's mission.

Mission Sixteen

We had an easy mission to a flying bomb site in the Calais area this morning. I was letting Lucky turn the aircraft around after the mission and we almost tore the tail off of *Betty's Revenge*. She hit the put-put. I'll bet Sanford, the crew chief, will really be mad.

We started on another mission this afternoon and number two engine of Denney's airplane went out just like the one on our ship the other day. That's two abortions in three days.

Mission Seventeen

July 7, Friday, 22:00:

What a mission today. Target: Leipzig, Germany.

I haven't seen so much flak since all my get-together. The boys said there was dense perpetual flak at the target. I heartily agree with them. There was a B-17 out of control over the city of Leipzig. The big bird was doing everything imaginable, whipping in the wind to then climb, sharp to right, to left, up, down. It was hard to tell what it was going to do next. It gives one the feeling of utter helplessness when a plane is not under their control. It's hard to describe the feeling that flak gives you. We just saw one chute come out of the plane. I wonder where the other nine boys went.

Bralley made some pictures today of the flak and stuff.

July 8, Saturday, 20:00:

I flew a practice mission as copilot for Gruman on a PFF camera mission. That PFF is a good thing if it works correctly. I rode back from Polebrook with Katz and Zimmerman in a command car. They had brought some pictures over.

I had a swell time this afternoon. I went to Oundle with Lt. Sutherland to play tennis. We certainly had a good time. Don took *along a bottle of sherry wine. Girls, women, and all drink over here. I feel little for refusing but that's my only choice.*

July 9, Sunday, 23:00:

I started out to go see Tom Lowrance this morning but was screwed out of use of a truck to go to Kettering. I attended chapel tonight.

Several of the boys were promoted today. Morin and McClung were among the lucky boys.

Lucketti and Morin are up at Leicester on pass. Morin will be surprised and Lucky will be pissed off because he's still a 2nd Lt. McClung is a little high tonight, celebrating his promotion. A little poker is in progress.

July 10, Monday, 21:00:

I slept most of the day today. Some of us went to Kettering today. I walked to the train station with S/Sgt. Tommie Fields and got mixed up in the Red Cross donut truck.

I got a report on some of my enlisted men and their pass in London. Smith and Smeallie were telling me about it tonight. Smeallie, Riep, and Bralley had the same hotel room. They had two or three quarts of Scotch and were really feeling tight. They got into a big fight and broke two or three chairs. Bralley tore his Bordeaux wound open. They're all good friends now but they look like a bunch of sad sacks. I have a pretty good bunch of boys but they really like to drink. Ivey and Burnett are the two dependable ones.

MISSION EIGHTEEN

July 11, Tuesday:

Let's quit this old stuff. They sent us to München, Germany, this morning. I mean to say, that was a long haul. The trip lasted eleven hours. I'll say, my old fanny was sore when we finally arrived here. At good old Deenethorpe. There was gobs of flak but thank goodness it was a little low. That is, the majority of it was.

We had a little excitement on the bomb run. I smelled some strange odor. I looked down and saw Morin's Gee box smoking. If there's anything that scares an airman, it's fire, and especially so when that black stuff is popping around out there.

Morin grabbed a fire extinguisher and started pumping. By that time everyone on the ship had smelled the smoke. Bud, were they excited. Bralley jumped up to help Morin and pulled his oxygen hose connection loose. We were at twenty-seven thousand feet and he passed out like a light.

Between the Gee box and reviving Bralley, Morin had his hands full. Bralley recovered just in time to salvo the bombs. Bralley said the last thing he remembered was trying to get to his parachute. We had a pleasant surprise when we arrived here at the barracks. Maj. Hinkle had torn some of the boys' beds up. That really makes a person think the world of his CO. Fly eleven hours and come in and find your bed on the floor.

Good man in the ETO. West Point man too.

July 11, 1944. Joel Clayton Thomas, the older brother of Betty Thomas, was enlisted into the army. He took basic training at Camp Wheeler and was assigned the job of rifleman in the 22nd Infantry of the 4th Army when his training was completed.

MISSION NINETEEN

July 12, Wednesday:
A nasty habit the higher-ups have. They sent us back to München today. The weather was really punk. We flew the entire bomb run through clouds. The two wing groups were abreast the lead group and dropped our bombs by command over VHF. Very accurate bombing. I don't see much sense in bombing nothing down there. I really don't care for killing all those people. The flak was right up there in the clouds with us today. The gunners must have gotten checked out yesterday. We had the photo's movie camera today; a person feels silly as all get out up here taking pictures.

This makes twenty-one hours I've flown in two days.

I received letters today.

July 13, Thursday, 20:00:
Was I pissed off this morning when they lifted that curtain in the briefing room. München again, only Rozzell was flying spare.

I found out something today. The town of München is Munich. I've been to Munich twice thinking it was some little place. I knew they had lots of flak there, now I see why. Oh well! I'm glad it was that way. Saved me a lot of sweating. I went to see the doc, Hardesty, sprayed throat.

181

July 14, Friday, 21:00:

The group stood down today.

Lucky and I went for a little bike ride tonight. We rode down to Brigstock and around. I hope my wife never asks me what's a Brigstock? I suspect I better hit the sack, we're going on another mission tomorrow. I was just thinking of the boys who came over here with us. There were fifty crew members, now there's only thirty left. Neil and Alberton have gone down, Neil at Leipzig. I don't remember where Alberton got it.

Grady and his crew flew the B-17 named Freckles, #42-107092, on July 13.

MISSION TO MUNICH

July 15, Saturday, 21:00:

The mission was scrubbed last night. McClung said it was going to be a rough, tough job. I don't care if they scrubbed them all. We went to Kettering for a little while tonight.

Mission Twenty

July 16, Sunday, 21:00:

We went back to Munich today and I knew it was Munich.

Those flak gunners over there are really checked out now. They have taken advantage of the practice they've been getting the past week, believe me. That Gee box caught fire again today at exactly the same place. They handled it in short order today though. Just another occurrence.

Clouds covered the target again today. I suspect we'll be going back. A lot of wasted effort. The target is an aircraft engine plant.

July 27, Monday, 21:00:

We flew a practice mission this afternoon. I was checked out as squadron lead.

I was joining the chow line this afternoon and happened to glance down the line and there stood my old classmate from Hendricks Field, Robert Sproul. He had just arrived at Benefield. He's in the 615th Squadron. Same old Sproul, if there's one man in the army that I appreciate, it's Sproul. He took all the ass-chewing at Hendricks Field. I'll never forget the hearty laughs we've had out of him. Here's hoping him the best of luck in the ETO. He'll need it.

One of the officers has him a little case all sewed up. Attempted rape

183

or so goes the latest rumor. There's a big, broad Red Cross dame here on the field. It was with her the guy had his deal. She ran over to the enlisted men's mess with just her slip on, holding her shoes in her hand. Man is slated to go home too. I hope it doesn't cause him any delay. It's okay if he wants to go home. I know I'd certainly like to go home.

MISSION TWENTY-ONE

July 18, Tuesday, 21:00:
   Another long haul. Today we went north over the North Sea, across Kiel to Peenemünde. The target was a producing factory for hydrogen peroxide or something like that. It's used in connection with jet-propelled planes. There's a big scare of these new planes.

   We led the second element of the low-squadron today. The flak was accurate over the target today. As we went in to bomb, we could look off to the left and below and see Sweden. Dear old neutral Sweden. If anything had happened we would have been over there in a jiffy!

   It was overcast when we came back to the field so we had to make an instrument letdown.

MISSION TWENTY-TWO

July 19, Wednesday, 21:00:

*I wish they'd quit giving us these soft targets. We bombed Augsburg,
Germany. I could say we were shot at Augsburg too. Rosie's Sweat Box
had it again today. They shot number three engine up today, there was a
large hole in the left wing and, of course, the usual many one-inch holes.
As we approached the field, number three engine went out. The moisture
control and prop control had been shot away. The cables were clanging
around the wheel. We led the hi-squadron.*

MISSION TWENTY-THREE

July 20, Tuesday, 21:00:

We led the low-squadron today. These frazzling missions are getting rougher and rougher. I'm afraid of that flak and I don't care who knows it. I like to have had it today.

We bombed Leipzig for the second time today. I hate to go back to these places twice. The second time is always twice as rough. Those boys don't need practice in the first place, but when they do get practice, they really give you the works. As we were going through some of the thickest, the cockpit seemed to explode. I looked up and the top of the cockpit was shattered. Fine glass was all over everything. I looked down and saw a gaping hole in the left side of the fuselage and looked farther to the right and saw where the piece had hit. There was a one-inch hole right through the supercharger control box. The piece missed my knee by about an inch. If I had had my feet on the rudders at that moment, I'd have had one less good knee. I thought my knee was hit anyway. It hurt all the way back down. When I arrived on the ground and found out it wasn't hurt at all, it quit its aching. It's funny how that thing hurt. Well, it wasn't exactly funny.

While on the bomb run, the deputy lead plane started throwing gasoline from under the wing at number two engine. In a few seconds, the spray of gasoline turned to a rich red flame that licked the entire length of the fuselage. The plane lost its position in the formation and dropped *behind and down. She then went out of control, recovered, and the flame seemed to go out. In a few moments though, the flame began again and Ivey reported it going down and then its explosion. It was Murgatroyd, flying deputy lead.*

I made some motion picture shots of the flaming plane. Boy, I'm worn-out, pooped, and don't care what happens. I'm really getting old with these missions. They're flying me too often. This flying and flak are getting me down. I've had enough of this crap. I'm ready for some rest. I want to get my missions in, but I want to be able to walk after I finish.

MISSION TWENTY-FOUR

July 21, Friday, 21:00:

We lead the hi-squadron on another one of those "milk runs." The target was the ball-bearing works of Schweinfurt, Germany. Ask anyone that's ever flown missions about Schweinfurt.

We were carrying incendiaries today. The group leader certainly wrung me out today. We screwed in and out of clouds all day. After going through some of the thickest flak I've ever seen on the bomb run, our group leader started descending trying to get under the clouds. At fifteen thousand feet, he gave up and took us through the thickest cloud around.

I lost sight of the formation. My airspeed froze, I had vertigo—well, everything happened. My wingman said the last time he saw me, I was going around 200 mph in a thirty-degree bank. I was pulling forty inches and 2,200 RPM, indicating 130. I'll bet we made close to 400 mph in those clouds. After seemingly ages, we broke out of the clouds, the airspeed thawed out.

We joined a B-24 outfit and came back with them. The B-24s brought us back safely. Our formation got shot. Those B-24 boys can smell that flak. They have too many hydraulic lines to be shot at. They came back home at the clip of 170 mph.

I was just about gone when we landed. I walked into interrogation and was given the wonderful news that I was grounded for flying fatigue.

About time. John Schultz told me I messed up his flying list. I should have told him to blow it out his operation's ASS.

I found out tonight that I had been grounded by Col. Bowman, CO of the field. He said four consecutive missions to Germany was enough for anyone. It was too much for Rozzell and crew. Lucky said I asked for the first-aid kit as I started on the bomb run today. The sky was literally black out in front. When we arrived, the black spots turned to popping red bursts. Whew! I hate that stuff. I don't see how anyone can go through that stuff thirty-five times. I'm glad I only have nine more missions to go. That's nine too many though. I decided a long time ago that I wanted to leave here.

July 22, Saturday, 21:00:

We went to see the flight surgeon this morning. We're going back on flying status tomorrow. I'm still tired and don't give a hoot whether I ever fly another mission or not. It's going to be a relief to go back to the states and fly with no one shooting at you, I'm telling you it will!

July 23, Sunday, 20:00:

Attended chapel again this morning. We walked to Kettering tonight. We had a load of fun at the cafe. There were five of us at the table. One of the boys, natural as anything, took out a needle and sewed a button on his jacket. The catch was that he didn't have a needle or a button. All of us sat there and watched him with the greatest concern. Everyone around gaped at us. I suspect they thought we were crazy. To be frank, their thoughts weren't far-fetched either. The condition is commonly known as "flak happy" in the ETO. We have the extreme condition. These fellows are doing a lot of talking in their sleep.

July 24, Monday, 12:00:

I think I'll go to Leicester with Morin this afternoon. I feel a lot better today. We have a forty-eight-hour pass. I've already spent twenty-four hours of it in the sack.

July 25, Tuesday, 21:30:

I got back from Leicester around 19:00 tonight. I had a nice time. I believe the trip did me some good. I'm relaxed a lot now.

Morin certainly has a cute girl up there. I talked to an Italian girl for a while tonight. She told me a story of her father and family. Her father had been interned in England and while being shipped back to Italy, his ship was torpedoed by an English boat. She thinks as much of the English as I. She can't stay out past 22:00 and can't leave Leicester without special permission. She is eighteen and has had to take care of her mother and four children.

Am I p-ed off. They've pulled two short missions since we left in support of the ground troops out of St. Lo. I hope they did a swell job. I hate to miss those short missions.

July 26, Wednesday, 22:00:

I slept all morning. We were briefed for a mission this afternoon but it was scrubbed. I was disgusted when I got in the briefing room. The mission was a short trip to bomb some oil storage at Paris. I missed the last two short ones and here I was flying spare on this one.

Capt. Kirkloft and his navigator, Lt. Pierce, are just back from the states. They put in twenty-five missions and went home and are back to do twenty-five more. They are sorry that they took the deal. They knew what it is over here and believe you me, they dread starting again.

I forgot to mention, Morin is a proud papa. His baby was born about five days ago. He's a big boy named Ronnie.

July 27, Thursday, 21:00:

We had another scrubbed mission this morning. Was I glad it was scrubbed! The target was Munich again. I wish someone would blow that place off the map. I don't want the job anymore though. I went over to the hospital to see McClung tonight and took the Victrola over to play some records.

MISSION TWENTY-FIVE

July 28, Friday, 22:00:

This was a pretty good mission today. It was easy to stay in formation, no clouds to fly through. There was plenty of flak but most of it was low and inaccurate. The clouds covered the target and we bombed PFF. My, but I hate to waste all that time and bombs. I don't trust instrument bombing.

MISSION TWENTY-SIX

July 29, Saturday, 21:00:

    This was a screwed-up affair today. The wing leader, Maj. Garland, had to abort and never did show up for assembly. The lead called up and said they were shooting green, green flares, so was everyone else in the sky. We managed to tag onto the right leader. We led the hi-squadron.

    The target was Merseburg again. Man, I hate to go to these targets the second time. Our wing was behind everyone else. One of the boxes turned around and came back to the field. That just left two boxes in our wing. Maybe I wasn't sweating. I just knew the fighters would attack us back there straggling. As luck would have it, they hit the wing just ahead of us. By the way they were talking, the fighters must have knocked half of their ships out.

    When we got to the target, clouds were covering it but smoke was boiling up through them so we bombed the smoke. Part of our bombs stuck on one stake. Smith climbed in the bomb bay and knocked them out one at a time. It takes a lot of guts to go in that open bomb bay six miles above the ground, with flak bursting, and kick out bombs. Good boy, Smitty. We took a lot of ribbing about all those houses we blew up with those bombs that dribbled out.

    We had a new CTG today. Bralley is grounded. His ears are bothering him. We nearly got the tail-end of our ship shot off today. They are going to put new elevators on her. She'll be flying in another day or so. Poor old Ivey really takes a beating back there in the tail. He's been hit two or three times.

I got a kick out of the boys on their radio coming back today. They've got to where they listen over VHF to aircraft in distress, just like it was a prize fight or something. One of the boys today had the nose blown off his ship, bombardier killed, navigator wounded, and he was about to bail the rest of his crew out. The boys were calling in all the news. The mad Russian (navigator) told us this morning that he could tell whether we were going on a bad mission or not by the amount of urine in the buckets in the latrine after briefing.

I loaned Petty five pounds to go to London with a blonde tonight. I hope he doesn't catch anything. I sweat my boys out.

July 30, Sunday, 20:00:

Attended chapel again this morning. Stayed on the sack most of the day. We're having a big laugh at one of our boys tonight. He went to London on his pass. He was looking for a piece of paper to write his girl's name on. He pulled a piece of paper from his pocket unmindedly and handed it to her to write her name. It was a "rubber" packet!

Mission Twenty-Seven

July 31, Monday, 22:00:

I wish someone would crush Munich but good. We went back down there today. We led the third element of the low-squadron. I sweated more today.

Our ship is still out for repairs. The first ship they gave us this morning was "Round Tripper," a ship with fifty missions. As I was pre-flighting, gas started pouring out the left wing. I was glad.

Then the next ship they gave us was "Fancy Nancy." She was on her fifty-third mission. Such an airplane I've never seen. All four engines were scaring me. Number one cyl. head temperature was high. I had to go all the way with the cowl flap open. Number two engine was running so rough I had to run most of the way in emergency rich; number three engine finally went out on the way back and I had to feather it. Number four engine tach fluctuated and finally went out entirely.

I was just glad to get that crate back on the ground. We struggled to stay in formation but when they started climbing from twenty-thousand feet to bombing altitude, I just couldn't make it so I motioned for my wingmen to go up without me; we straggled behind and caught the formation just in time to drop our bombs. The flak is rough at Munich. If you don't believe it, go there. I don't want to anymore.

I'll be glad when my airplane is fixed. She gets in shape, we fly her a mission, and get her all shot up. I'm sweating out these airplanes more than I am the flak. I've seen a lot of flak and know we can go through it, but the sorry planes I don't like.

Morin said the CTG (Ellis) that we had today laid down on the floor when the flak started coming up. This was his first mission. His voice quivered all day. We left the formation at the coast and came back by ourselves. We beat the formation back in on three engines.

Mission Twenty-Eight

August 1, Tuesday, 22:00:

We had another late briefing this morning. For a good change, we went to France. We bombed an airfield at Chartres, France. We had orders to post hole the airfield.

The airfield housed the new Me 263 jet-propelled airplane. Everyone is jet crazy around here. Every contrail they see is a jet plane. We led the low-squadron today. Low airspeed by the leader screwed us up all day. There was a few clouds and contrails. There was too much flak.

My classmate Robert Sproul went down today. It makes a fellow feel low when one of his buddies goes down. I don't like to write about them but Sproul was such a close buddy. He and Melofchik were flying fifth and sixth positions of the low box. At the target, a piece of flak or prop wash rendered Melofchik's airplane uncontrollable. His plane came over on Sproul's nose and chewed the front of Sproul's plane out. Melofchik's plane pulled on up and Sproul's wreck broke his plane into in the middle. Melofchik's plane went down in two pieces. Sproul flipped over on his back into a spin. The last time they saw Sproul, he was clawing at the top glass in the cockpit. When our friend goes down—well, I hope I can forget this stuff. I'll never be able to though. A fellow will never forget those planes spinning and burning. You know there's ten good men in there.

I'll always remember Sproul at Hendricks. Goldbrick Sproul. You

201

couldn't help but like him. Never worried about a thing. I introduced him to Chaplain Burke about two missions before he went down. This was Sproul's fourth mission. Before every mission, Sproul would come around me and say, "Rosey, you only have twenty-four more missions than me." I'm afraid he'll never catch up with me now though. God bless him.

I'm really sweating out the last few missions. I've never been so worried in my life. I can see the end so clearly now. I mean, we're sweating. I'd like to get a haircut and my pay if they'd give me a day off. I haven't had a haircut in about three weeks. I need it and bad.

August 2, Wednesday, 21:00:

The group was stood down today.

I got out of the sack early to get a haircut. The shop was already full so Rosey still looks like a mongrel. However, I did manage to get my pay, fortunately. I bought a hundred-dollar war bond and sent it to Betty. They're having a big bond drive here in the 8th Air Force to help the boys that are fighting the war.

I played a game of darts with a new copilot, Hafley. It was the first time I had played in a long time.

I have five more missions to go. (Five too many!) Fog season is starting here in England. I wrote Mother a letter tonight and ended it by saying "so long." I didn't like that so I put in "good night" and finally ended up saying "I'll be seeing you." Sounds more heartening.

Poker games have started in the barracks. They generally last for ten or fifteen days after payday.

The boys said I was talking in my sleep last night. It's kind of humorous to hear some of the other boys sleep talk. They talk about every-thing—flak, fighters and one boy was talking to a nurse.

Mission Twenty-Nine

August 3, Thursday, 22:00:

We got in another mission today. The target was the Marshaling yards at Strasbourg, France. The mission wasn't too rough. We flew spare and filled in number two of the hi-squadron.

We ran over some rough flak en route to the target. A hunk of it went through the leading edge of the right wing, knocking a hole about a foot long and two inches wide. That was a nasty-looking wound out there.

This was the first time we'd flown our own ship in three or four days and she's out of commission for another day or two. Only four more missions to go. (Four too many!)

Mission Thirty

August 4, Friday, 21:00:

Another long haul today. Except for the great length of time we flew, the mission was practically a milk run. We bombed storage houses for the jet-propelled planes. We led the low-squadron. The bomb load consisted of incendiaries. Ninety percent of the bombs flew within five hundred feet of the MPI. I mean to say, your old tail-end gets sore on these tiresome runs. We could see dear old Sweden again today.

Taylor finished his missions today. He flies out right away. They threw him in the pond beside the mess hall. They picked his frail fanny up and tossed him into the middle of the thing. I get a kick out of Taylor. He used to come around after briefing and give me flak instruction. He'd have it all figured out as to whether we should turn steep or shallow off the bomb run. He's pretty scary after his Berlin deal. He goes wild when we get in that stuff, forgets all about the formation and skids all over the sky.

I have three more missions to go. (Three too many!) I can see the end of the missions out there now. Maybe you think I'm not worrying. When I had so many missions to go, I didn't worry so much.

It'd really make me mad to get shot down on my last few missions. Quit talking like that, Rozzell, no one's going to shoot you.

Grady and his crew flew aircraft #42-97869 named "Hula Girl" on this and the next mission.

MISSION THIRTY-ONE

August 5, Saturday, 21:00:

Getting closer and closer to the finish now, only two more to go. *(Two too many!)* The target today was some underground oil storage tanks at Nienburg, Germany. Did we hit it?

I really love to bomb oil. She spouts and burst into vivid red chutes of fire. BLOODTHIRSTY. She was blazing when we left. We were carrying eight one-thousand-pound bombs, the heaviest load we've ever carried. That's four tons. The mission was practically a milk run. We led the low-squadron.

We could see Hamburg and Hanover. Hamburg is one big black burnt place. The oil there caused a lot of fires. If we'd bombed PFF today, we were going to bomb Hanover. Brother, that's no picnic.

The flight surgeon grounded my crew today. Lucky is jittery and on edge. I leaned over to look at an airplane on our right wing and my flak helmet fell off on the throttles and practically in his lap. He turned loose of everything and started out of the airplane. He thought the cockpit had been hit again. He really cursed me for dropping that big flopping helmet. I don't blame him, but it scared me nearly as bad as it did him. *(Two more to go, two too many!)*

209

August 6, Sunday, 20:00:

If I must say so, this was a very good day to be grounded. The boys went to the outskirts of Berlin.

I feel low tonight. One of my best buddies got killed today. He was flying in the tail of my airplane, Rosie's Sweat Box. T/Sgt. Garon was hit in the rectum and bled to death in a little over two minutes. The big piece of flak came up through the tail, into him, and lodged up in his entrails. Garon yelled that he was hit on the interphone. Jones, the waist gunner, looked back and noticed that there was some blood on his tail. Jones told Oscehirt, the pilot, that Garon was hurt and that he was going back to see about him.

When Jones arrived in the tail, Garon was already dead. He was frozen at his guns. They tried to get him loose but to no avail. They couldn't even get his hands off to take his pulse, so they put their hands inside his clothes and felt for his heart. It wasn't beating. His eyes were already set. Nearly everyone on the ship tried to get him loose. They had to land with him back there. After they came down from altitude, his blood thawed out and was still dripping when the airplane taxied to the dispersal.

They had a lot of trouble getting Garon out. One big brute of a medic finally climbed over Garon and got in the rear. By putting his feet in his abdomen and pushing, he was able to break Garon loose. Bright, copilot, said Garon looked just like wax. All the blood drained from his body in just a few minutes.

Boys get killed nearly every day, but it doesn't bother one so much until a close friend gets it. It stirs a fellow up and makes him want to kill every German that ever lived. Bright, his copilot, seems to be disturbed considerably. This was the first mission that the crew had flown in quite a while. I feel sorry for Ivey. It's going to be hard on him climbing into that bloody tail.

Ivey had had all kinds of narrow escapes as it is. He has been hit two or three times. That tail has dozens of holes in it. The plane has a new elevator. Well, it's just a sieve back there. I'm glad we just have two more missions to go.

We lost an entire crew today. Saurwald in "Round Tripper." Saurwald flew on my left wing and put in his first mission yesterday. This was his second trip. That plane, Round Tripper, was on its fifty-first mission. I won't have to fly it now, I know.

I went to communion tonight. Ivey was over there. I imagine he was plenty scared.

August 7, Monday:

We didn't even get up to fly this morning. The other boys went and were scrubbed. Garon's brother, a sailor, came to see him last night. He had to walk from Peterborough (twenty miles) to get here to find out that his brother was dead. Can you imagine how he feels? Missed seeing his brother by twelve and a half hours. I hate to think about it.

We had a little talk by Col. Bowman this afternoon. He talked like they might raise the number of missions. I hope they don't try anything like that. I was supposed to go on pass tomorrow but Oscehirt's crew is going to Garon's funeral tomorrow so I'll have to fly in his place.

MISSION THIRTY-TWO

August 8, Tuesday, 21:00:

An ideal mission, I must say. The mission was in support of the ground troops just before they made a mad rush at the Germans. This kind of bombing proved effective the last push they made. In fact, they haven't stopped yet. We carried thirty-eight one-hundred-pound bombs but didn't get to drop them. Dust covered the target. Our lines were one thousand yards from the target. The low box dropped their bombs with good results. The high box did a disastrous thing — the bombs fell on our lines. That's no good.

It happened like this. They overshot their target in the first place. The lead ship, Maj. Maupin and Capt. Ball, got a direct hit by flak. They had a fire in the bomb bay and cockpit, so on instinct, they salvoed their bombs. Naturally, the rest of the formation dropped with him thinking he was bombing the target. The lead ship went down. Some of the men were reported out in chutes. I hope they made it okay and I hope too many of our men weren't killed. One more mission to go. (One too many!)

The Eighth Air Force Historical Society in their Narrative-Official Air Force Mission Description described the incident:

"Mission 531: 681 B-17s and 100 P-51s are dispatched to bomb enemy troop concentration and strong points S of Caen; 25 Canadian soldiers are killed and 131 wounded by short bombing . . . 7 B-17s are lost, 4 damaged beyond repair and 294 damaged; 8 airmen are KIA, 15 WIA and 35 MIA . . ."

This was Mission 125 for 614th Squadron of the 401st. Their records were concise:

"The lead aircraft of the high box had just reached the Canadian lines when it took a direct flak burst and burst into flames, killing four of the crew. The bombs were released in the emergency and, in consequence, the whole of the box released their bombs at the same time, bombing the Canadian front line. Twenty-five Canadian soldiers were killed and 131 wounded in this regrettable incident."

The 614th Squadron did not bomb because of smoke and dust obscuring the target. On the mission to Hautmesnil, Grady and his crew flew aircraft #42-31863 named "Miss B. Haven."

MISSION THIRTY-THREE

For their final mission, Grady and his crew flew aircraft #43-
37602 named "Lady Vivian."

August 9, Wednesday, 21:00:
*Day of days for Rosie. I finished my combat tour today. Yep, she's
all through, and am I happy. Strange as it may seem, I don't feel as
hilarious as I should. Instead of the feeling of hilarity, I have a feeling of
uneasiness. I can't seem to relax, I can't realize that I won't have to get
up at the break or before dawn tomorrow, eat a breakfast of powdered
eggs, go to briefing, and climb into Rosie's Sweat Box, take off through
the fog and mist, climb to altitude and assemble, begin the long trek
across to Nazi Germany, wear a clinging, aggravating oxygen mask for
a six- or seven-hour stretch, sweat out flak and fighters, fight a big box
of an airplane to keep in formation for nine or ten hours.*

*This all seems like a wonderful dream. Maybe it will be a realization
when I lay in the sack in the morning and watch the other boys go out.
I don't like to sit back and watch the other fellows go out, but I've seen
enough, so if they'll let me sit here, that's what I'll do.*

*We finished our missions in record time for this group. In two
months and nine days, we flew thirty-three missions and were credited*

for two. Just to think that within a month from now I might be back with Betty, my folks, and the other dear people I know. It's just too much for Rosey to believe.

I had to buy the barracks a quart of Scotch tonight for finishing my missions. It cost around twenty dollars. I owe them a quart for promotion but I'm afraid they'll never see it.

Six of my crew finished with me today — Morin, Burnett, Smeallie, Riep, and Ivey. Smith needs two, Bralley needs six more. Smith lost out when he was in the hospital with a sore throat. At least that was what he told me. His throat wasn't sore though. It was something else. The commodes are loaded in London.

I didn't get thrown in the pond tonight. I think I'll get by without a dunking now. The boys weren't at the mess hall when I slipped in. Did I scoot out of there when I finished eating.

Talking about a perturbed fellow, you should have seen me this morning when they pulled the curtain. There, staring me in the face, was my old friend Munich. Sweat and more sweat.

We didn't go there though. We might as well have gone there, they didn't change their mind until we were almost there. We were over Belgium when we started ascending into the clouds. We flew in the clouds for a clocked hour. That's some of the hardest as well as most dangerous and most straining work that you'll ever do. Imagine flying in clouds with one thousand other planes when you barely can distinguish a plane seventy feet away. Our formation made it okay though. After seemingly ages, they announced that we were letting down to bomb a target of opportunity. Suits me fine. I don't want to go to Munich!

We ended up by bombing some railroad yard in Luxembourg. I'm going over to get the DFC tomorrow. Tonight I'm going to write a letter to my wife and mother that I've been wanting to write for a long two months. Darling, I'm all through.

Grady's last mission was mission #126 for the 614th Squadron of the 401st. The squadron report reads:

"Lt. C. C. Lincoln led the low box to bomb the airfield at Munich. Heavy clouds up to twenty-five thousand feet and dense contrails made it impossible to keep the formation together, so a target of opportunity was selected and the Squadron struck the marshaling yards at Luxembourg with excellent results. No enemy aircraft were encountered and the flak was scattered, meager but fairly accurate."

The six 614th crews on this mission were:

#42-31081: 1st Lt. C. A. Lincoln and crew
#42-97145: 1st Lt. T. D. Carroll and crew
#42-31863: 2nd Lt. L. R Hayes and crew
#42-107151: 2nd Lt. H. P. Silverstein and crew
#42-97478: 2nd Lt. P. W. Finney and crew
#42-97602: 1st Lt. W. G. Rozzell and crew

Grady's crew for the mission:

CP 1st Lt. Humbert Lucketti
N 1st Lt. B. J. Morin
CTG S/Sgt. Brown A. Bailey
RO T/Sgt. Major A. Burnett
TT T/Sgt. Donnan R. Smeallie
BT S/Sgt. Herman R. Riep
TG S/Sgt. George W. Ivey
WG Sgt. William M. Smith

August 10, Thursday, 21:00:

Eight of my crew were awarded the Distinguished Flying Cross for extraordinary achievement this evening. Col. Bowman made the presentation. He was twitching and so were we. I didn't sleep well last night. I can't relax. Maybe in a day or two the strain will be over.

Maj. Maupin, who went down the day before yesterday, is already back. He bailed out in our lines and they flew him back. He looks like he has had a horrifying experience, which he has. Four of his enlisted men weren't so lucky. They're dead. All four of the officers got out okay though. The extent of their wounds is unknown.

McKeon, a fellow who went down at the last Leipzig raid, is already back. He set the record for coming out of Germany.

August 14, Monday, 09:00:

Well, it looks like our stay here is short now. We received our orders two or three days ago. I've cleared most of the field. All I have left is a little packing to do. Lucky finished about two days ago. He's leaving with us. Good deal.

August 15, Tuesday, 21:00: 12th RCD, Charley, England.

We said farewell to the boys at 401st this morning. Caught a GI truck to Kettering, a train to Charley, and a bus to here. This place isn't bad at all. I can see now where I'm going to get a little extra sack that I've been missing the past two weeks. I'm in a little six-by-ten room with a Capt. Bombardier. He's leaving tonight though, that will give me a little extra elbow room.

He gave me some comforting news. He had just returned from the dispensary and had found out that he had scabies. More things happen to me. Oh well, if I get 'em, I get 'em. Let's hope not. I've been feeling the things crawling on me already though.

There's more captains and majors floating around here. There's one thing I've noticed about those fellows here. They don't look as young and fresh as the boys we came over with. You don't hear much about combat here. No one wishes to talk about it. Everyone is happy to be going home. I know just how they feel. Just think, I may be home in three weeks. You think about it, it's too much for me.

The chow here seems to be okay. I'm going to eat and sleep. I had this diary all sealed to turn in but I decided to bring it on up here with me. Well, I think I'll try the sack.

August 16, Wednesday, 22:00:

Ah! What a life. Didn't sleep but ten hours last night. I'll do better tonight though. We went to the orientation lectures this morning, which consisted of the chaplain, surgeon and venereal disease, and a corporal from special services. The chaplain made an impressive talk. He told of the problem of thousands of pregnant girls here in England. They certainly go all out for the prevention of disease here. They even have the MPs carrying prophylaxes.

I was told some kind of hard news this afternoon. I was talking to Showers, a classmate of mine at Hendricks in 43-I. It seems as though every one of my buddies at Hendricks is gone. I mean down in Germany or dead. Jimmy Sasser, the closest buddy I had all the way through training, was killed buzzing a few weeks ago. My two room-mates, Roth and Roeder, went down. Rupert and Schomp, two basket-ball players at Hendricks, are down. Among the others are Siewert, Skymanski, Nesen, Lloyd, Sproul (401st), Alterton (401st), McKeon (401st), Newt (401st), Murgatroid (401st), Ball (401st), Kilmer (401st), Wilson (401st), Sovenwald (401st).

I suspect this is all the price of war. Very expensive though. That hurt when they told me about Sasser. It just doesn't sound right, and I'm not going to believe it. I know it's true though.

McKeon, one of the boys I mentioned above, is back. I was talking to him just before I left. He was shot down at Leipzig but had control of his plane and made it back over into France. He bailed out at eight hundred feet. He seemed to like it over there. Said he lived on steak and wine. He said there were two diets: bread and water or steak and wine. He preferred the steak and wine. McKeon doesn't have to fly anymore.

Another buddy of mine, Filmyer, was shot down at Bordeaux. He bailed his crew out in Spain and they're all back flying again—that is, all but the tail gunner and bombardier. The tail gunner was killed when flak blew the tail almost completely off. The bombardier is shocked and refused to fly anymore. He tried one mission after he came back. The whole crew protested violently. You can tell they've had a rough time. I, for one, will be glad when this thing is over. I don't think it will last over another month or two. The fellows were flying in support of the ground troops when I left. They were blowing up roads and bridges behind the Germans so they couldn't retreat so fast.

I've been reading a book on the personal traits of Abraham Lincoln. Some fellow, Lincoln.

August 17, Thursday, 21:00:

Had a short physical this afternoon consisting of a short arm and immunizations record check. For once I went through without having a shot. I was watching the fellows having their baggage checked this afternoon. One of the inspectors tried to take my watch. Some nerve. I'll hide the thing when I get my baggage checked. We'll be here for about ten or twelve more days I think.

August 18, Friday, 21:00:

I had a rather interesting trip to Liverpool today. Lucky and I went on a bus tour given by special services. After looking at the bombed buildings in Liverpool, I think it would have been a rest to live in London during the Blitz. This place was hit, and I mean hit. I wonder what Berlin looks like. We were conducted by an old member of the Rotary Club.

We went under the river through the tunnel. Very modern to be in England. We visited the ATS camp where the airraid system control is. They claim it is what saved England during the Battle of Britain. They do have a wonderful system.

After having lunch at the British Consul Building, we went to an AA gun site. Frankly, I'm glad I saw the guns after I finished my missions rather than before. I didn't realize the amount of work we were making the Germans do when they were shooting at us. There's a lot of valuable equipment tied up in those guns. Those fellows took a lot of pride in their guns and actually wanted the Germans to come over so they could try them out.

Posta told me tonight that Sasser killed eleven men when he crashed. Jimmy was a swell buddy of mine. I really feel sorry for Freddie, his wife, and Sally Moore, his sister-in-law.

August 22, Tuesday, 21:30:

Today I have been at the 12th RCD for exactly a week—and, may I add, a week too long. Yep, I'm ready to go home now. I've rested enough. Rosey feels like a new man (boy). Now, I can say "man" in four days now—for in four days, I will have reached the ripe old age of twenty-one. Yes, sir, I'm just about to grow up. Just right for the draft.

They have three types of men coming through the Replacement Center: Happy Warrior, R&R, RAD. The Happy Warriors are the boys who have completed their missions and are going home to stay. The R&R are the fellows who have completed twenty-five missions and are going home for rest and recuperation and then come back for more missions. The RAD are the fellows who are banged up and will be removed from active duty when they arrive in the states.

Some of my buddies left today. Some are leaving tomorrow. I suspect my days in the ETO will be few, at least I hope so. I was on the mail-censoring detail today. The ground personnel seem to admire the reformers here by the description that I've seen in their letters. One young man really told his wife about—well, about a little thing. Here's hoping Rozzell's name is on that shipping list tomorrow.

ROSIE'S SWEAT BOX
LAST MISSION

Rosie's Sweat Box was a model B-17G aircraft manufactured by Lockheed/Vega Aircraft Corp in Burbank, California. The plane was delivered to Tulsa and into service of the US Army Air Force on March 22, 1944, and given the serial number #42-97872. It was assigned to the 401st Bomb Group and delivered to Deenethorpe on June 1, 1944. Grady Rozzell and his crew took the plane on its first mission on June 11, 1944. That mission was to Munich, Germany, and was a rough, sweat-filled mission. The sweat from that mission was the inspiration for the name "Rosie's Sweat Box." The plane completed nineteen missions. Grady and his men flew her in eight of them.

On the early fall Sunday morning of September 17, 1944, Second Lt. Francis E. Cook and his B-17 flight team were making final preparation for a bombing run to Holland. The crew was made up of nine men. In addition to Lt. Cook, the pilot, there was his copilot, 2nd Lt P. H. Clark; navigator, 2nd Lt. C. R. Werner; bombardier, 2nd Lt. F. W. Jorgensen; radio operator, Cpl. W. E. Weston; engineer/top turret gunner, Cpl. W. H. Dahlin; ball turret gunner, Cpl. J. L. Page Jr.; tail gunner, Cpl. W. J. Ambrogette; and waist gunner, Cpl. J. R. Browning.

The crew of Lt. Cook had been assigned to the 614th Squadron of the 401st Bomb Group for a very short time and had taken part in only one mission prior to this one. Their first mission had taken place a week earlier on September 10 and was flown to Gaggenau, Germany, to destroy the Daimler-Benz aircraft engine plant at that city. On that mission, Lt. Cook piloted the B-17G named "Miss B. Haven."

The mission number for men involved from the 614th Squadron on that September 17 morning was 144; the target was Groesbeck. Briefing started at 0300 hours. The target details called for the target to be Siegfried Line fortification and artillery. The specific objective of the operation was to take out German flak batteries prior to the great airborne invasion of Holland by Allied troops. The group, including the crew of Lt. Cook, was assigned a target in a wooded area near Groesbeck, where a concentration of enemy tanks and gun positions was located. The invasion was known as "Operation Market Garden."

There were a total of fifty-one crews briefed for this mission, featuring Lt. Col. W. T. Seawell, group air commander. The crews from Deenethorpe started their engines at 0515 hours and were in line to taxi at 0530 hours. The take-off for the 401st began at 05:45 with an estimated time to return to base of 1113 hours.

Lt. Cook and his crew were assigned the aircraft flying under the nickname of "Rosie's Sweat Box" for the September 17 mission. This was to be the twentieth mission for the plane which was named and flown principally by 1st Lt. Woodville Grady Rozzell.

At 0606 hours, Rosie's Sweat Box crashed while attempting to take off. The plane fell heavily, approximately 750 yards off the end of the runway. The plane exploded, spreading debris to both sides and onto Weldon Road. With the exception of Cpl. W. J. Ambrogette, the crew members were mortally wounded in the explosion. Cpl. Ambrogette was the tail gunner and was thrown free of the burning plane. He was treated by the medical staff immediately but died of his wounds in a matter of hours.

The details from 401st microfilm said:

"The aircraft failed to clear the hedge at the end of the main east-west runway and crashed onto the main Weldon to Oundle road. The explosion was instant and devastating, as was to be expected with 6,000 pounds of "Frag" bombs and 2,400 gallons of aviation fuel. It seemed miraculous to those that rushed to the scene to find someone still alive, sitting by the side of the road. Sadly, he proved to be fatally injured and died later that day. This was the tail gunner, Cpl. W. J. Ambrogette, who was buried at the American Cemetery at Madingley, Cambridge."

On December 5, 1943, one of the thirty original B-17 aircraft to arrive at Deenethorpe from the US also crashed on takeoff. That was the plane named "Zenodia-El-Elephanta." It was the only other plane to crash while leaving the base during its operation as a US Army Air Force facility. All of the crew of that aircraft were able to escape without serious injury. The only report of casualty was a cow and a fire tender, which were too close to the crash site.

Betty Rozzell visited Deenethorpe in 2013. After Dad died, Mother told me during a chance conversation, "Grady always promised to take me to England to see the base he flew out of." I found quickly that the rest of her family was as innocent of her desire to see the place in England that Dad had known as home during the war as I. Our family was fortunate enough to be able to take her at the age of eighty-nine to Deenethorpe. We were able to show her London and Paris and the D-Day beaches, and she proved to have plenty of stamina to appreciate every minute of the trip.

A year or so after we returned, I asked her what she remembered most about the place we visited. She quickly replied, "That long lonesome airstrip. Grady talked about being lined up on that airstrip and how he had to keep both feet pushed as hard as he could on the brakes, how hard it was to hold that plane back when he had it at full throttle, waiting on the flare so he could take off. They were sending them off every fifteen seconds and they had to get all the speed they could to get in the air by the time they reached the end.

"I don't understand how they kept from running into each other," she said. Crashes at takeoff and at formation join-up were a very real concern. The early morning in East Anglia was usually cloudy. Once they were in the cloud, they could hope to get high enough to be in the clear before the formation leader released colored smoke grenades to gather in their respective groups.

Mother surprised me when she said, "I was really glad we were able to visit the crash site of Grady's plane." That one bothered me for a while. Dad was home before the Sweat Box crashed on takeoff, but I am sure she heard many stories about the plane and the crash.

AFTER THE WAR

When his regular service ended, Dad and Mother went back to the Chattanooga area. They lived with his parents at 4011 Twelfth Avenue in East Lake for a short time. He found a lot available on Missionary Ridge and, with the help of the GI Bill, was able to build and occupy a small house there.

A friend offered him a twelve-acre tract of land in Chickamauga, Georgia. He now had a family and a desire to be a farmer. He moved the family into an existing house on the land in Chickamauga. The family expanded to include not only the son, David, but daughters Terri, Carol, and Peggy. He grew corn and beans on the land and usually raised a steer, which provided hamburgers for the winter.

Dad was never without a horse. A farm is not complete without a dog. He brought home every breed, size, and shape of dog. We loved them all. He had a friend who was raising registered beagles and Dad decided we would raise beagles. The county had an active beagle club which held regular field trials. We became members. After that, most every Saturday morning, Dad and I would load up a few beagles and drive somewhere to hunt rabbits.

In the fourteen years Dad and Mother owned the Chickamauga land, they worked constantly to upgrade the place. Dad worked after-hour carpentry jobs with his father to provide funds and, with the help of Mother and children, did most of the labor. One of his after-hour jobs was the remodel and upgrade of a dental office in Rossville. Dad was in constant need of dental work. He thought the family should have a better relationship with dentists than he had known. The family was introduced to his dentist friend.

During the early part of the family stay in Chickamauga, Dad took a job as superintendent of a crew constructing an addition to the woolen mill in Rossville. The job lasted two years. While there, Dad got to know the management team of the factory. He also went back to the University of Chattanooga to complete the engineering degree he had started prior to the war. The construction project and an opening in the engineering department of the factory occurred about the same time and Dad accepted the job as an assistant plant engineer in the Burlington Industries Company. He would be an engineer for the rest of his working life.

Dad was always an athlete. He loved any competition. During the family stay in Georgia, he was a member of any softball team which asked him to participate. The factory had organized leagues for basketball, badminton, softball, and baseball. He played all of them. He developed a passion for golf and tennis and took on all comers. It was not enough that he personally participated in things outside our home. He supported his children to do the same. "Pushed us" would be too strong a term, but he made sure we knew he appreciated our efforts. We were exposed to sports, music, and academics. He bought a piano and encouraged each of us to learn at least the basics.

Dad took his church seriously. Attendance in church on Sunday morning and afternoon was mandatory. He was a member and served in several churches as either Deacon, Sunday school teacher, and/or treasurer. I was present a few times when he discussed scripture and church life with friends, but I do not remember any personal conversation with him about any religious matter. I mentioned the fact to a sister who said simply, "His religious communications were to live the example of being a good man, a good person, and a good parent. He was fabulous at communicating those things."

After being out of the service and flying a year or so, he felt a need to fly. He joined the Tennessee National Guard unit stationed in Chattanooga when he discovered they had an opening for a pilot. The planes were single-engine observation planes for the artillery, but they were planes and he was paid to fly them.

A year or so into his stay with the guard, his unit got a helicopter. Neither he nor the other pilots in his unit had ever flown a helicopter. After a few attempts, they all flew it. One Saturday morning, Dad and one of his pilot buddies were getting flight time in with the helicopter. They brought the thing to our house and landed it in our pasture. We had very few neighbors, for what I figured was several miles. By the time the blades stopped turning on the helicopter, our pasture was full of people. They were all walking and I have yet to figure out where they all came from.

With all he did outside our house, Dad still found time for his children. He taught us to love animals and to love each other. He made a strong attempt to help us love school. He had a particular love of math. That one was a hard sell. One trait I marvel at is, he managed to be at our kitchen table every afternoon at 5:45.

He could never have accomplished these things without a very strong partner. Mother ran the business of family. She handled all things financial, knew where every dime went. She kept the family in food and sewed our clothes. She kept the lights on and the water flowing. She made the doctor appointments and kept up with the schools. She kept the ship afloat.

In Swannanoa, Dad took a bigger role in the community. His largest contribution was to the local schools. In 1977, he was elected to the Buncombe County School Board. He served his last year of that term as the board's chairman. In 2007, on the strength of his contributions to its programs, he was inducted into the Sports Hall of Fame of Owen High School. He followed and supported faithfully the sports activity of his four children and six grandchildren, who graduated from OHS.

Dad was, at his core, a builder. As long as he was physically able, he did his share of the hammering, cutting, and lifting. When he was slowed by age, he still did the planning and supervision. His drawing board was always covered with projects. He was continually planning and drawing additions to his house, to a neighbor's house, to a church building, or to anyone who asked him for suggestions. He loved to draw plans. Many of the plans were completed in his wonderful mind. Life, to him, was a work in progress.

Acknowledgments

Thank you to everyone who offered advice and was so kind in their support and encouragement during the process of writing this book.